Population

OPPOSING VIEWPOINTS®

Other Books of Related Interest

Population

OPPOSING VIEWPOINTS®

Charles F. Hohm, Department of Sociology
San Diego State University, *Book Editor*

Lori Justine Jones, Department of Sociology
San Diego State University, *Book Editor*

Shoon Lio, Department of Sociology
University of California, Riverside, *Book Editor*

David L. Bender, *Publisher*
Bruno Leone, *Executive Editor*
Bonnie Szumski, *Editorial Director*
David M. Haugen, *Managing Editor*

OPPOSING
VIEWPOINTS®
SERIES

Greenhaven Press, Inc., San Diego, California

Cover photo: PhotoDisc, Inc.

Library of Congress Cataloging-in-Publication Data

Population : opposing viewpoints / Charles F. Hohm,
Lori Justine Jones, and Shoon Lio, book editors.
  p.   cm. — (Opposing viewpoints series)
An anthology of previously published articles, completely up-
dated from the 1995 edition.
Includes bibliographical references and index.
Summary: Considers opposing opinions on various issues
concerning world population including problems of rapid
growth, the effects of population on the environment, and ways
of decreasing human fertility.
  ISBN 0-7377-0291-5 (pbk. : alk. paper). —
ISBN 0-7377-0292-3 (lib. : alk. paper)
  1. Population. [1. Population.] I. Hohm, Charles F., 1947– ,
Jones, Lori Justine, 1961– , Lio, Shoon, 1963– .
II. Series: Opposing viewpoints series (Unnumbered)

HB883.P67 2000
  304.6—dc21   99-056750
                                                           CIP

Greenhaven Press, Inc., P.O. Box 289009
San Diego, CA 92198-9009

> "Congress shall make
> no law...abridging the
> freedom of speech, or of
> the press."

First Amendment to the U.S. Constitution

The basic foundation of our democracy is the First Amendment guarantee of freedom of expression. The Opposing Viewpoints Series is dedicated to the concept of this basic freedom and the idea that it is more important to practice it than to enshrine it.

Contents

Why Consider
Opposing Viewpoints?

*"The only way in which a human being can make some
approach to knowing the whole of a subject is by hearing
what can be said about it by persons of every variety of
opinion and studying all modes in which it can be looked
at by every character of mind. No wise man ever acquired
his wisdom in any mode but this."*

John Stuart Mill

In our media-intensive culture it is not difficult to find differing opinions. Thousands of newspapers and magazines
and dozens of radio and television talk shows resound with
differing points of view. The difficulty lies in deciding
which opinion to agree with and which "experts" seem the
most credible. The more inundated we become with differing opinions and claims, the more essential it is to hone
critical reading and thinking skills to evaluate these ideas.
Opposing Viewpoints books address this problem directly
by presenting stimulating debates that can be used to enhance and teach these skills. The varied opinions contained
in each book examine many different aspects of a single issue. While examining these conveniently edited opposing
views, readers can develop critical thinking skills such as the
ability to compare and contrast authors' credibility, facts,
argumentation styles, use of persuasive techniques, and
other stylistic tools. In short, the Opposing Viewpoints Series is an ideal way to attain the higher-level thinking and
reading skills so essential in a culture of diverse and contra-
dictory opinions.

In addition to providing a tool for critical thinking, Opposing Viewpoints books challenge readers to question
their own strongly held opinions and assumptions. Most
people form their opinions on the basis of upbringing, peer
pressure, and personal, cultural, or professional bias. By
reading carefully balanced opposing views, readers must directly confront new ideas as well as the opinions of those

with whom they disagree. This is not to simplistically argue that everyone who reads opposing views will—or should—change his or her opinion. Instead, the series enhances readers' understanding of their own views by encouraging confrontation with opposing ideas. Careful examination of others' views can lead to the readers' understanding of the logical inconsistencies in their own opinions, perspective on why they hold an opinion, and the consideration of the possibility that their opinion requires further evaluation.

Evaluating Other Opinions

To ensure that this type of examination occurs, Opposing Viewpoints books present all types of opinions. Prominent spokespeople on different sides of each issue as well as well-known professionals from many disciplines challenge the reader. An additional goal of the series is to provide a forum for other, less known, or even unpopular viewpoints. The opinion of an ordinary person who has had to make the decision to cut off life support from a terminally ill relative, for example, may be just as valuable and provide just as much insight as a medical ethicist's professional opinion. The editors have two additional purposes in including these less known views. One, the editors encourage readers to respect others' opinions—even when not enhanced by professional credibility. It is only by reading or listening to and objectively evaluating others' ideas that one can determine whether they are worthy of consideration. Two, the inclusion of such viewpoints encourages the important critical thinking skill of objectively evaluating an author's credentials and bias. This evaluation will illuminate an author's reasons for taking a particular stance on an issue and will aid in readers' evaluation of the author's ideas.

As series editors of the Opposing Viewpoints Series, it is our hope that these books will give readers a deeper understanding of the issues debated and an appreciation of the complexity of even seemingly simple issues when good and honest people disagree. This awareness is particularly important in a democratic society such as ours in which people enter into public debate to determine the common good.

Those with whom one disagrees should not be regarded as enemies but rather as people whose views deserve careful examination and may shed light on one's own.

Thomas Jefferson once said that "difference of opinion leads to inquiry, and inquiry to truth." Jefferson, a broadly educated man, argued that "if a nation expects to be ignorant and free . . . it expects what never was and never will be." As individuals and as a nation, it is imperative that we consider the opinions of others and examine them with skill and discernment. The Opposing Viewpoints Series is intended to help readers achieve this goal.

David L. Bender & Bruno Leone,
Series Editors

Greenhaven Press anthologies primarily consist of previously published material taken from a variety of sources, including periodicals, books, scholarly journals, newspapers, government documents, and position papers from private and public organizations. These original sources are often edited for length and to ensure their accessibility for a young adult audience. The anthology editors also change the original titles of these works in order to clearly present the main thesis of each viewpoint and to explicitly indicate the opinion presented in the viewpoint. These alterations are made in consideration of both the reading and comprehension levels of a young adult audience. Every effort is made to ensure that Greenhaven Press accurately reflects the original intent of the authors included in this anthology.

Introduction

"The possibility must be considered seriously that the number of people on the Earth has reached, or will reach within half a century, the maximum number the Earth can support in modes of life that we. . . will choose to want."
—*Joel Cohen*, How Many People Can the Earth Support?

"The ultimate resource is people—skilled, spirited, and hopeful people who will exert their wills and imaginations for their own benefit, and so, inevitably, for the benefit of us all."
—*Julian Simon*, The Ultimate Resource

Entering into the population debate is like stepping into a conversation that has been going on for centuries. Since ancient times people have argued over what the size of their communities should be. The formal scientific study of human populations—demography—can be traced back to an eighteenth-century English clergyman, Thomas Malthus. In his 1798 treatise, *An Essay on the Principle of Population*, he first expounded the basic idea that rapid rates of human population growth might be a serious problem.

According to Malthus, humans' natural ability to reproduce exceeds their ability to feed themselves, and population growth inevitably leads to famine and wars for food and other resources. Malthus's ideas have been refined over the years (and some have been discredited), but many demographers still subscribe to his basic premise—that rapid population growth is inherently destructive.

At the same time, there were those who disagreed with Malthus. For example, Karl Marx, whose writings began the socialist movement, believed that war, famine, and other forms of human suffering are caused by the inequities of capitalism rather than overpopulation. In the twentieth century, advances in food production eased many people's fears that humanity will become unable to feed itself. According to the United Nations Food and Agriculture Organization, the average crop yields of rice, wheat, and maize have doubled since the 1960s. This Green Revolution, as the advances are often called, has bolstered many people's faith that scientific progress can solve other problems associated with overpopulation as well.

Today, those who believe that rapid population growth is inherently harmful are called Malthusians, while those who believe that science, technology, and social justice can provide for any size population are called Utopians. Both of these worldviews are continually being developed and debated. They each offer their own ideas about how population growth affects economic growth, the environment, and other quality-of-life concerns, and they each offer their own approach to population issues.

Although Malthus was, for religious reasons, firmly opposed to contraception, one "Malthusian" approach to population growth has been the movement for birth control in Europe and North America. The birth control movement, led by Margaret Sanger in the early 1900s, was a forerunner to the twentieth-century movement for family planning and population control. Today, family planning programs have expanded all over the world. A "population establishment"— a network of agencies, including the United Nations Population Fund and other organizations that promote family planning throughout the world— is thriving.

Sanger primarily advanced a socialist feminist ideology of equality for women. However, some of Sanger's ideas, including her infamous words "more children from the fit, and less from the unfit," were adopted by racist eugenicists who believed they could improve the white race through the control of human mating. The Holocaust and other instances of genocide throughout the world gave a perverse meaning to the term "population control," and the modern population establishment is always careful to explain that their goal is to enable people to make informed choices about whether or not to have children.

In this sense, the movement to control population is intertwined with the history of the women's movement. Beginning with Margaret Sanger, who coined the term "birth control," the early women's rights movement promoted women's control of their own bodies. This idea—that women and their partners must be able to make choices about if and when to have children—is known as reproductive freedom. Many population control advocates believe that women who lack adequate access to contraception lack reproductive freedom. Thus the population establishment seeks to promote reproductive freedom by providing women in developing nations with access to contraception, safe abortions, and other family planning services.

The United Nations *World Population Plan of Action* maintains that population policies should be consistent with "internationally and nationally recognized human rights." However, many people charge that some population control measures conflict with women's reproductive freedom. Nations with low birthrates may provide incentives, such as tax breaks or child care services, for families to have children. These are termed pronatalist policies. On the other hand, crowded nations may encourage or even force women to use contraception, undergo sterilization, or have abortions. Policies aimed at decreasing the fertility rate are called antinatalist policies. Whether pronatalist or antinatalist, many people believe that all forms of population control constitute an unjustifiable intrusion of government power into the lives of its citizens.

The planet's population is growing. The authors in *Population: Opposing Viewpoints* debate how serious the problem is and what to do about it in the following chapters: The Historical Debate: Is There a Population Problem? How Will Population Grow in the Twenty-First Century? How Serious a Problem Is Overpopulation? Can Nations Control Population Without Violating Individuals' Reproductive Freedom? In examining this global issue, it is hoped that readers will gain a fuller understanding of the demographics that underlie so many other current social issues, such as the role of government in people's private lives, the state of the global environment, and the many challenges that the international community faces in helping Third World nations achieve social stability and economic prosperity.

CHAPTER 1

The Historical Debate: Is There a Population Problem?

Chapter Preface

In 1798 an English clergyman, Thomas Robert Malthus, wrote *An Essay on the Principle of Population*, postulating that population tends to grow much faster than the food supply and concluding that human misery will always result from this natural law. A pious scholar who had studied philosophy and economics as well as theology, Malthus wrote to refute the views of such contemporaries as William Godwin and the Marquis de Condorcet, who promoted a rosier view of mankind's development. While his more optimistic colleagues tended to agree with Johann Peter Süssmilch ("the father of German demography") that population growth was a necessary precondition to economic and social prosperity, Malthus drew on the work of another English clergyman/scholar, Joseph Townsend, who felt that discouraging population growth was a necessary function of the state.

In a sense, the debate was between those who considered more people an asset and those who considered them a liability, or at least a burden. That debate took a political twist half a century after Malthus published his *Essay*, when Frederick Engels (best known as coauthor, with Karl Marx, of *The Communist Manifesto*) entered the fray. Engels argued that Malthus's theory of population had been contrived by capitalists to explain and rationalize poverty. Charging that the whole concept of overpopulation was a myth, Engels contended that reorganizing society on communist lines would end poverty.

The debates on population often are based on predictions—dire or rosy—about the effects of having more or fewer people on Earth. The viewpoints in this chapter provide a historical perspective of the opening salvos of that debate.

> *"The Almighty will bless, protect, and maintain a people that obeys His command to multiply and populate the earth."*

The State Should Encourage Population Growth

Johann Peter Süssmilch

The work of German statistician/demographer Johann Peter Süssmilch (1707–1767) is not well known to the English-speaking world, primarily because none of his books have been translated into English. Süssmilch was a first-rate thinker, how-ever, and his major contribution to population studies was his extensive work on demography (the study of population)—the first such attempt in any language. The first edition of his book *The Divine Order in the Transformation of the Human Race as Demonstrated Through Birth, Death, and the Multiplication of the Same* was published in 1741. Süssmilch was very pronatalist and thought that one of the primary duties of the state was to promote marriage and childbearing, following the rules he sets forth in this viewpoint.

As you read, consider the following questions:

1. What obstacles does Süssmilch say the state should try to remove so that citizens can marry at an early age?
2. What should the state do to enhance childbearing within marriage, according to the author?
3. Why does the author believe the state should try to keep its citizens from emigrating to other countries?

Excerpted from "Removing Obstacles to Population Growth," by Johann Peter Süssmilch, translated by Eileen Hennessy. Reprinted, with the permission of the Population Council, from *Population and Development Review*, vol. 9, no. 3, September 1983, pp. 521–29.

Rule 1: The State Should Remove Obstacles Delaying or Preventing Marriage

A [State] must first combat all forcible hindrances to marriage and reproduction, insofar as it lies within [its] power, and to the extent permitted by Providence and the relations among empires in the world. A State must therefore not keep any person from marrying, be he minister, layman, or soldier. War is a fearful destroyer of marriages and the population. Can the [State] then sufficiently abominate it according to its deserts? The fight against the plague often rewards prudence with a successful outcome. Can any expense and effort then be spared in keeping this grave enemy and waster of countries from its borders? As plague and war can quickly plunder the fruits of many previous years and the increase of humankind, so on the contrary sound and peaceful ages are most advantageous to the population, if the sources are not obstructed by other causes. From the annual surplus of births in the Prussian lands, which in an average year amounts to 24,000, it is clearly evident that every year of peace is a new conquest.

We must then distinguish two mainstays in the performance of the great duty to replenish the population, which same must be brought to the greatest possible perfection. They are, the plough and the loom. Many people perhaps hear these two words with contempt, but they are the principal supports of the State and the sources of power and wealth. By the plough I mean the science of using the land and soil of a State in such manner that is most beneficial to the populace and, consequently, to power and wealth. It can easily be adjudged that much intelligence, experience, and effort are part of such science. By the loom I understand all types of labor usually included under the terms manufactures and works. Both things together occupy the hands and diligence of a Nation, and no country can exist and flourish without well-ordered diligence. The cultivation of the land takes precedence over all other things. It is and must be the basis for manufactures and commerce, because it provides the raw materials for processing, and hands must therefore serve it. It is thus a grave error if preference is given to manufactures over agriculture and if the former are operated to the prejudice of the latter. . . .

Rule 2: The State Should Eliminate All Impediments to Marital Fertility

The fertility of marriages varies, being in some places seven or sometimes eight children for every two marriages, in some places and at some periods nine children. This difference is of great importance, and warrants full attention on the part of the State, since the extent and the speed of replenishment of the population are dependent thereon. . . .

The first and most important cause [of this difference] resides in the fact that in a heavily populated country most males marry late, and the women, including rural folk, also marry almost too late, often not before the age of 30, and many still later. The years most appropriate for procreation slip by, and instead of ten or more children such marriages produce barely four or five, particularly since peasant women nurse their infants for a long time. If more people can be enabled to marry, they will also marry sooner. When in a province five births per marriage can be counted, this is a sign that there are more, and earlier, marriages in that province than in one in which four or even three children are produced by each marriage. If more people are to enter into matrimony, at an earlier age, then sufficient encouragement and adequate maintenance must be provided. . . . Improvements in agriculture, manufactures, and commerce are also involved herein.

Fear of the dangers of childbirth has a great influence on marital fertility. The State should therefore seek to alleviate this fear, insofar as is possible, by good means of assistance. It would be wise to have a good and inexpensive school for the training of midwives in every State.

The unequal marriages between young men and women over 40, and between young maidens and decrepit elderly men, are against the intention of the Creator of Nature and against the primary goal of matrimony, and they represent a disadvantage for the State; so they should be forbidden, and not permitted without dispensation and payment of a contribution, in proportion to means, to the widows' or marriage fund.

Parents who have many children must be given substantial financial support by the State, particularly those parents who live in large cities and are in the employ of the State, and who are devoid of means because in the city sustenance and upbringing are more costly, a certain general outlay of money is unavoidable, the children cannot be clothed and brought up in the same way as farm children; impecunious civil servants are seldom able to set anything aside, those who have some money must expend their wealth when they have many children, and, lastly, the functionaries whom the State will continue to need will for the most part also be drawn from among the children of the citizens and inhabitants of the large cities. . . .

The Biblical Injunction

God said: "Let us make mankind in our image and likeness; and let them have dominion over the fish of the sea, the birds of the air, the cattle, over all the wild animals and every creature that crawls on the earth.". . . Then God blessed them and said to them: "Be fruitful and multiply; fill the earth and subdue it."

Holy Bible, King James Version, Genesis 1:26–29.

Luxury is an impediment to marital fertility and fertility in general, as well as to marriage. . . .

The long nursing of children is a great impediment to marital fertility, particularly in the countryside, as we have already noted. But can it be limited by law, especially when it is done out of fear of the danger of childbirth, and when adequate means of assistance for diminishing that danger have not been set up? Here again, the best remedy would be to extend the assistance given to parents of many children also in the countryside. A peasant who has six, eight, and more children increases not only the security of the State but also its revenues, certainly in proportion, more than the farmer who has few or no children. Beer and brandy must be obtained for baptisms and marriages, from cities that pay excise taxes; the more children there are, the more fabric, shoes, books, hats and so on will be needed. Such a father therefore contributes more to the treasury of the State, and hence he is more deserving of certain advantages than is another. The same sort of encouragements can easily be discovered for the peasant as well. . . .

Rule 3: The State Should Help
Preserve the Lives of Its Citizens

Many, if not most, of [the lives of] people [who die prematurely] could be saved if the State were sufficiently watchful, if it controlled evil practices, if it allocated the necessary funds for medical science. . . . I should like to note my inability to understand why more heed is not paid to the science that has as its object the precious thing that is human life. Quite good and almost adequate institutions exist almost everywhere for the very necessary instruction and the development of the human spirit through truth. The necessary attention has also been paid to the practice of law in civil society. Individuals are maintained in both fields at the expense of the State. Only the maintenance of human life seems to me everywhere to have been ignored. Some steps are undertaken, but insufficiently and inadequately. Physicians are maintained for the poor in the cities, but only in the large cities. But what is one physician for a place that has 50,000 or 100,000 or more inhabitants? Physicians are appointed for entire districts, to which, however, they attend only when dangerous diseases appear among men or animals, or when a murder occurs and they must investigate the case and the causes of a death and give their opinion thereon. But how poorly are they compensated? And how can a renowned practitioner in a city attend to illnesses in villages that are often six and more miles away? Everything I have observed in establishments connected with human life is in question. Yet better provisions appear to be simple. Hitherto medical science and the physician appear to have devoted themselves almost exclusively to the wealthy, who are able to pay them for their effort. There are preachers everywhere. How easy and how inexpensive it would be to establish, in good locations at two-mile intervals, a preacher who also has some knowledge of medical science, with reasonable compensation! The best minds could be sought out for the purpose, and with slight effort they could be enabled to devote three years to medicine, with somewhat less attention paid to the learning of oriental languages and Greek, if these have not already been learned in school. . . .

Rule 4: **The State Must Endeavour to Keep Its Subjects at Home and Attract Foreigners, If Necessary**

Devising ways to keep people [from leaving for other countries] is an obligation. A native-born subject is in most cases and respects better than two colonists. He is habituated to the customs and the way of life, and during time of war the fatherland can command greater loyalty from him. The first thing, then, is indeed to reflect whether sustenance for more families might not be created through improvements in agriculture, manufactures, and commerce? Whether there are not defects in the existing distribution of farmland, and whether same could not be redressed? Whether the domains of the princes and the extensive holdings of the large landowners, nobles, monasteries, convents, and cities should not be divided and broken up and populated with more peasants? . . . When manufactures fail, the worker leaves the country for places where he hopes to find sustenance; when they recover, he returns, or foreigners come in. Thus great intelligence and undiminished reflection and study are needed in order to determine whether everything that could and should be done is in fact being done? Whether the needs of a country can be met by its own subjects, or whether families are being induced, through negligence, to seek their sustenance in foreign countries, with consequent support and promotion of the power and riches of those countries? The history of the kingdoms of the world provides us with remarkable examples of this. . . . Seville and Spain as a whole have lost through the collapse of the wool and silk manufactures and are still losing because of the continuing neglect, since they are obliged to purchase their primary needs and fabrics from England, Holland, France, and Italy, and even from the Germans, although the country has the raw materials and they are moreover of the best quality. . . .

When there is reasonable freedom, security, and justice in a country, where good morals and fashions prevail, where the arts and sciences flourish, where the government pays heed to increasing the means of subsistence and to creating various sources of food, the people can be secured against emigration and foreigners will certainly be moved to enter the country. And, what is at all times the most important thing, the Almighty will bless, protect, and maintain a people that obeys His command to multiply and populate the earth; all such a people does will be successful.

> *"Speculation apart, it is a fact, that in England, we have more than we can feed, and many more than we can profitably employ under the present system of our laws."*

The State Should Discourage Population Growth

Joseph Townsend

The English Poor Laws that provided the public relief from the end of the 1500s well into the 1800s generated heated debate among intellectuals of the time, among them Joseph Townsend (1739–1816). Townsend was a man of many talents—physician, geologist, Methodist clergyman. His *Dissertation on the Poor Laws, by a Well-Wisher to Mankind* was published in 1786, twelve years before Thomas Malthus's famous *Essay on the Principle of Population*. Though Townsend's work is void of the moralizing that appears in Malthus's later work, it makes many of the same points. A principal point, which he makes in the following viewpoint, is that welfare destroys the motivation to succeed and leads to excess population and misery.

As you read, consider the following questions:
1. How are population levels dependent on the quality of the land, according to the author?
2. What three remedies does Townsend list for countries where population is pressing on the land's ability to produce? Which two does he call "natural" remedies?
3. How does giving resources to the poor encourage overpopulation, in Townsend's view?

Excerpted from Section 9 of Joseph Townsend's *Dissertation on the Poor Laws*, 1786. Reprinted, with the permission of the Population Council, from *Population and Development Review*, vol. 8, no. 3, September 1982, pp. 608–11.

On the subject of population we have had warm disputes, whilst some have lamented that our numbers are decreasing, and others with confidence have boasted that our population has rapidly advanced; all seeming to be agreed, that the wealth of a country consists in the number of its inhabitants. When industry and frugality keep pace with population, or rather when population is only the consequence of these, the strength and riches of a nation will bear proportion to the number of its citizens: but when the increase of people is unnatural and forced, when it arises only from a community of goods, it tends to poverty and weakness. In respect to population, some countries will reach their ne plus ultra [highest possible point] sooner, and some later, according as they surmount the obstacles which impede their progress. This period can be retarded by improvements in agriculture, by living harder or by working more, by extensive conquests or by increasing commerce.

People Are Dependent on the Land

The cultivation of rice in China enabled them to feed some millions of people, more than could have been maintained by any other grain; whereas in the highlands of Scotland, where neither rice nor yet wheat will grow, the inhabitants soon became a burthen to the soil. Their chief dependence for supporting the present population is on frugality, and constant, steady, unremitted labour, without any hope of being able to advance their numbers. Oatmeal and water, with a little milk, is their common food, and to procure this they work as long as they can see. They till the soil; they watch their cattle; and, at their leisure hours, they spin all the linen and the woollen which their families consume.

The Romans, even when they had lost their domestic industry and habits of economy, were able to feed their increasing citizens by tribute from the distant provinces, as the Spaniards do by purchasing provisions with the gold and silver of Peru. The Dutch have no other refuge but in good government, industry, and commerce, for which their situation is most favourable. Their pastures are rich, but not sufficient to maintain half the number of their inhabitants, who are employed and fed by every nation upon earth, but reside in Holland for the convenience of the water-carriage, the security of their persons, and the protection of their property.

Remedies for Excess Population

When a country is so far advanced in population as to be distressed for food; and when the forementioned resources have been exhausted, it has then reached its utmost limits; and in such a case, against increasing want there can be two remedies only which are natural, and one unnatural: for either none must marry, but they who can maintain a family, or else all who are in distress must emigrate. If these natural remedies are rejected, it can remain only for the poor to expose their children the moment they are born, which is the horrid practice adopted in the richest country upon earth [England] to preserve the community from famine. With regard to celibacy, we may observe, that where things are left to a course of nature, one passion regulates another, and the stronger appetite restrains the weaker. There is an appetite, which is and should be urgent, but which, if left to operate without restraint, would multiply the human species before provision could be made for their support. Some check, some balance is therefore absolutely needful, and hunger is the proper balance; hunger, not as directly felt, or feared by the individual for himself, but as foreseen and feared for his immediate offspring. Were it not for this the equilibrium would not be preserved so near as it is at present in the world, between the numbers of people and the quantity of food. Various are the circumstances to be observed in different nations, which tend to blunt the shafts of Cupid, or at least to quench the torch of Hymen. In many parts of Europe, we see multitudes of both sexes, not from policy, but from superstition and religious prejudice, bound by irrevocable vows of chastity. In other parts we hear of numbers who are compelled to spend their days in a seraglio, where it is not to be expected that all should be prolific; whilst in consequence of this unjustifiable practice, a corresponding number must pass through the world without leaving a representative behind them. But in every country, at least on this side of the Atlantic Ocean, we find a similar effect from prudence; and without the assistance of either a seraglio, or a convent, the younger branches of the best families have been left to wither. In every country, multitudes would marry, if they had a comfortable prospect for themselves, and for their children; but if all should listen to this call of nature, deaf to a louder call, the whole world in a few years would be distressed with famine. Yet, even in such a case, when it is impolitic that all should marry, this should be wholly left to every man's discretion, and to that balance of the appetites which nature has established. But if, notwithstanding the restraints of distress and poverty, they who are not able to maintain a family will yet marry, there can be no resource but in emigration. In the highlands of Scotland, when the inhabitants became a burthen to the soil, they tried every possible expedient; and, when all others failed, their young men with reluctance turned their back upon a country which was not able to support them. It is well known that their emigrations are considerable. They do not issue forth in assembled multitudes, like swarms from the northern hives of old; nor do they, like a torrent, overflow and desolate the adjacent countries; but, like the silent dew, they drop upon the richest pastures, and wandering to the remotest corners of the earth in quest of food, with the industry of bees they collect their honey from the most luxuriant flowers. These active, hardy, and laborious people, are to be found in the temperate, in the torrid, and in the frigid zones, in every island, and on every habitable mountain of Europe, Asia, Africa, and America. Yet in their native country, the numbers never fail: the supply is constant. Now, if, instead of collecting for themselves, wherever food is to be found, these wanderers had been equally supported on their barren mountains by contributions from the more fertile vallies of the South, can we imagine that the births in Scotland would be fewer than they are at present? The overflowings of their population might have been accelerated, but could not thereby have been retarded. Having no contributions from the South, they have quitted their country, and made room for others. We are told, upon the best authority, that in the highlands of Scotland, a woman will bring twenty children into the world, and rear only two. Had she sufficient food for more, more would live. The women there, like the women in all countries which are come to their utmost height of population, are more prolific than the soil. To provide more food on their bleak and barren mountains, is beyond a question. But if now, to rear these twenty children, a poor's rate were to be collected in more fertile countries, yet in countries which are fully peopled in proportion to their labour, and to the produce of the soil, is it not evident, that the scarcity and distress would only be transferred, and that the children of the South must die, that the children of the North might live? But, supposing these should live; yet at best they could only take the place of those that died, and more women in the North would increase and multiply, till they felt the same degree of pressure which they feel at present. Neither Switzerland nor the coast of Africa, are depopulated by emigrations, because the quantity of food in each remains unaltered. It is with the human species as with all other articles of trade without a premium; the demand will regulate the market.

Giving Resources to the Poor Encourages Overpopulation

By establishing a community of goods, rather by giving to the idle and to the vicious, the *first* claim upon the produce of the earth, many of the more prudent, careful, and industrious citizens are straitened in their circumstances, and restrained from marriage. The farmer breeds only from the best of all his cattle; but our laws choose rather to preserve the worst, and seem to be anxious lest the breed should fail! The cry is, Population, population! population, at all events! But is there any reasonable fear of depopulation? We have seen that corn upon an average has been considerably cheaper since the commencement of the present [eighteenth] century, than it was for an equal term before; yet wages have been raised in the proportion of six to four, and the rent of land is doubled. May we not infer from hence, that the produce of the soil must have increased nearly in the same proportions. If we consider the improvements which have been made in agriculture, by clearing woods, inclosing wastes, draining morasses, laying the common fields in severalty, and making roads; by the introduction of clover, saintfoin [an

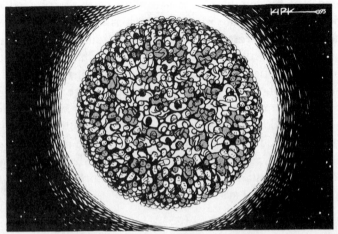

OUR BIOLOGICAL CLOCK IS TICKING

Reprinted with permission of Kirk Anderson.

herb grown for forage], turneps, and potatoes; by the break-ing up of extensive downs; and by the superior skill of the present race in the management of all sorts of land, with re-spect to stocking, manuring, cropping, not forgetting their superior weight of capital to work with; we shall cease to wonder at this vast increase of produce. But is it possible that the produce should be thus increased, and not the people also who consume it? We need not desire any man to visit Lon-don, Norwich, Bath, Bristol, Hull, Liverpool, Leeds, Wake-field, Manchester, and Birmingham: we need not call upon him to view our mines of coal, copper, lead, iron, and tin, with all the new manufactures which depend on these; but let him, at least, count our flocks, and calculate the quantity of corn produced by recent improvements in our tillage; then let him ask himself if our population is increased.

Whilst food is to be had, there is no fear of wanting people. But should the population of a country get beyond the produce of the soil, and of the capital engaged in trade, how shall these people find employment? Whenever this shall be the case, the evil will increase, and the capital will go on constantly diminishing; like as in private life, when a gentleman breaks in upon his principal to pay the ordinary expences of his family. When a trading nation is obliged to spend more than the revenue which is derived from commerce, and not from accident, but as the effect of some abiding cause, exceeds continually the profit of its trade, without some substantial reformation, the ruin of that nation will be inevitable. Should the capital itself accumulate, the interest of money would be lowered, the demand for labour would increase, and the superlucration [excessive profit] on this increase of trade would continue to enlarge the capital. Speculation apart, it is a fact, that in England, we have more than we can feed, and many more than we can profitably employ under the present system of our laws.

> *"The power of population is indefinitely greater than the power in the earth to produce subsistence for man."*

Overpopulation Is a Serious Problem

Thomas Robert Malthus

In the most famous work on population ever written, *An Essay on the Principle of Population* (1798), Thomas Robert Malthus (1766–1834) attacked the English Poor Laws as an ill-thought-out way to reduce poverty in England. In fact, he argued, public relief only results in stimulating population growth and making the situation worse. In the following viewpoint, Malthus states that two kinds of checks, positive and preventive, work to keep population from growing indefinitely. Late marriage was one of Malthus's preventive checks. It is interesting to note that Malthus practiced what he preached: This onetime country parson waited to get married until he was thirty-nine (when he became a professor of history and political economy), and he limited himself to three children, only one of whom lived to maturity.

As you read, consider the following questions:
1. What are the mathematical growth rates of population and of food production, according to Malthus? What problems does he infer from these rates?
2. What "positive" checks to population growth does the author describe?
3. According to the author, what are the "preventive" checks to population growth?

Excerpted from Thomas Robert Malthus, *An Essay on the Principle of Population* (1798).

I have read some of the speculations on the perfectibility of man and of society with great pleasure. I have been warmed and delighted with the enchanting picture which they hold forth. I ardently wish for such happy improvements. But I see great, and, to my understanding, unconquerable difficulties in the way to them. These difficulties it is my present purpose to state, declaring, at the same time, that so far from exulting in them, as a cause of triumph over the friends of innovation, nothing would give me greater pleasure than to see them completely removed.

A New View of an Old Argument

The most important argument that I shall adduce is certainly not new. The principles on which it depends have been explained in part by David Hume, and more at large by Dr. Adam Smith. It has been advanced and applied to the present subject, though not with its proper weight, or in the most forcible point of view, by Mr. Alfred Russel Wallace, and it may probably have been stated by many writers that I have never met with. I should certainly therefore not think of advancing it again, though I mean to place it in a point of view in some degree different from any that I have hitherto seen, if it had ever been fairly and satisfactorily answered.

The cause of this neglect on the part of the advocates for the perfectibility of mankind is not easily accounted for. I cannot doubt the talents of such men as William Godwin and the marquis de Condorcet. I am unwilling to doubt their candour. To my understanding, and probably to that of most others, the difficulty appears insurmountable. Yet these men of acknowledged ability and penetration, scarcely deign to notice it, and hold on their course in such speculations, with unabated ardour and undiminished confidence. I have certainly no right to say that they purposely shut their eyes to such arguments. I ought rather to doubt the validity of them, when neglected by such men, however forcibly their truth may strike my own mind. Yet in this respect it must be acknowledged that we are all of us too prone to err. If I saw a glass of wine repeatedly presented to a man, and he took no notice of it, I should be apt to think that he was blind or uncivil. A juster philosophy might teach me rather to think that my eyes deceived me and that the offer was not really what I conceived it to be.

In entering upon the argument I must premise that I put out of the question, at present, all mere conjectures, that is, all suppositions, the probable realization of which cannot be inferred upon any just philosophical grounds. A writer may tell me that he thinks man will ultimately become an ostrich. I cannot properly contradict him. But before he can expect to bring any reasonable person over to his opinion, he ought to shew, that the necks of mankind have been gradually elongating, that the lips have grown harder and more prominent, that the legs and feet are daily altering their shape, and that the hair is beginning to change into stubs of feathers. And till the probability of so wonderful a conversion can be shewn, it is surely lost time and lost eloquence to expatiate on the happiness of man in such a state; to describe his powers, both of running and flying, to paint him in a condition where all narrow luxuries would be contemned, where he would be employed only in collecting the necessaries of life, and where, consequently, each man's share of labour would be light, and his portion of leisure ample.

I think I may fairly make two postulata.

First, That food is necessary to the existence of man.

Secondly, That the passion between the sexes is necessary and will remain nearly in its present state.

These two laws, ever since we have had any knowledge of mankind, appear to have been fixed laws of our nature, and, as we have not hitherto seen any alteration in them, we have no right to conclude that they will ever cease to be what they now are, without an immediate act of power in that Being who first arranged the system of the universe, and for the advantage of his creatures, still executes, according to fixed laws, all its various operations.

I do not know that any writer has supposed that on this earth man will ultimately be able to live without food. But Mr. Godwin has conjectured that the passion between the sexes may in time be extinguished. As, however, he calls this part of his work a deviation into the land of conjecture, I will not dwell longer upon it at present than to say that the best arguments for the perfectibility of man are drawn from a contemplation of the great progress that he has already made from the savage state and the difficulty of saying where he is to stop. But towards the extinction of the passion between the sexes, no progress whatever has hitherto been made. It appears to exist in as much force at present as it did two thousand or four thousand years ago. There are individual exceptions now as there always have been. But, as these exceptions do not appear to increase in number, it would surely be a very unphilosophical mode of arguing, to infer merely from the existence of an exception, that the exception would, in time, become the rule, and the rule the exception.

Assuming then, my postulata as granted, I say, that the power of population is indefinitely greater than the power in the earth to produce subsistence for man.

Population Growth, Geometric; Food Supply, Arithmetic

Population, when unchecked, increases in a geometrical ratio. Subsistence increases only in an arithmetical ratio. A slight acquaintance with numbers will shew the immensity of the first power in comparison of the second.

By that law of our nature which makes food necessary to the life of man, the effects of these two unequal powers must be kept equal.

This implies a strong and constantly operating check on population from the difficulty of subsistence. This difficulty must fall some where and must necessarily be severely felt by a large portion of mankind.

Through the animal and vegetable kingdoms, nature has scattered the seeds of life abroad with the most profuse and liberal hand. She has been comparatively sparing in the room and the nourishment necessary to rear them. The germs of existence contained in this spot of earth, with ample food, and ample room to expand in, would fill millions of worlds in the course of a few thousand years. Necessity, that imperious all pervading law of nature, restrains them within the prescribed bounds. The race of plants, and the race of animals shrink under this great restrictive law. And the race of man cannot, by any efforts of reason, escape from it. Among plants and animals its effects are waste of seed, sickness, and premature death. Among mankind, misery and vice. . . .

Preventive and Positive Checks to Population Growth

A foresight of the difficulties attending the rearing of a family acts as a preventive check, and the actual distresses of some of the lower classes, by which they are disabled from giving the proper food and attention to their children, acts as a positive check to the natural increase of population.

England, as one of the most flourishing states of Europe, may be fairly taken for an example, and the observations made will apply with but little variation to any other country where the population increases slowly.

Preventive Checks in England

The preventive check appears to operate in some degree through all the ranks of society in England. There are some men, even in the highest rank, who are prevented from marrying by the idea of the expenses that they must retrench, and the fancied pleasures that they must deprive themselves of, on the supposition of having a family. These considerations are certainly trivial, but a preventive foresight of this kind has objects of much greater weight for its contemplation as we go lower.

A man of liberal education, but with an income only just sufficient to enable him to associate in the rank of gentlemen, must feel absolutely certain that if he marries and has a family he shall be obliged, if he mixes at all in society, to rank himself with moderate farmers and the lower class of tradesmen. The woman that a man of education would naturally make the object of his choice would be one brought up in the same tastes and sentiments with himself and used to the familiar intercourse of a society totally different from that to which she must be reduced by marriage. Can a man consent to place the object of his affection in a situation so discordant, probably, to her tastes and inclinations? Two or three steps of descent in society, particularly at this round of the ladder, where education ends and ignorance begins, will not be considered by the generality of people as a fancied and chimerical, but a real and essential evil. If society be held desirable, it surely must be free, equal, and reciprocal society, where benefits are conferred as well as received, and not such as the dependent finds with his patron or the poor with the rich.

These considerations undoubtedly prevent a great number in this rank of life from following the bent of their inclinations in an early attachment. Others, guided either by a stronger passion, or a weaker judgment, break through these restraints, and it would be hard indeed, if the gratification of so delightful a passion as virtuous love, did not, sometimes, more than counterbalance all its attendant evils. But I fear it must be owned, that the more general consequences of such marriages, are rather calculated to justify than to repress the forebodings of the prudent.

Domestic Virtue and Happiness for All

A more simple-minded virtuous man, full of domestic affections, than Mr. Malthus could not be found in all England. . . . The desire of his heart and the aim of his work were that domestic virtue and happiness should be placed within the reach of all, as nature intended. He found, in his day, that a portion of the people were underfed; and that one consequence of this was a fearful mortality among infants; and another consequence, the growth of a recklessness among the destitute which caused infanticide, corruption of morals, and, at best, marriage between pauper boys and girls, while multitudes of respectable men and women, who paid rates instead of consuming them, were unmarried at forty, or never married at all. Prudence as to the time of marriage, and making due provision for it, was, one would think, a harmless enough recommendation under the circumstances.

Harriet Martineau (1831), quoted in D.V. Glass, ed., *Introduction to Malthus*, 1953.

The sons of tradesmen and farmers are exhorted not to marry, and generally find it necessary to pursue this advice till they are settled in some business, or farm that may enable them to support a family. These events may not, perhaps, occur till they are far advanced in life. The scarcity of farms is a very general complaint in England. And the competition in every kind of business is so great that it is not possible that all should be successful.

The labourer who earns eighteen pence a day and lives with some degree of comfort as a single man, will hesitate a little before he divides that pittance among four or five, which seems to be but just sufficient for one. Harder fare and harder labour he would submit to for the sake of living with the woman that he loves, but he must feel conscious, if he thinks at all, that should he have a large family, and any ill luck whatever, no degree of frugality, no possible exertion of his manual strength could preserve him from the heart rending sensation of seeing his children starve, or of forfeiting his independence, and being obliged to the parish for their support. The love of independence is a sentiment that surely none would wish to be erased from the breast of man, though the parish law of England, it must be confessed, is a system of all others the most calculated gradually to weaken this sentiment, and in the end, may eradicate it completely.

The servants who live in gentlemen's families, have restraints that are yet stronger to break through in venturing upon marriage. They possess the necessaries, and even the comforts of life, almost in as great plenty as their masters. Their work is easy and their food luxurious compared with the class of labourers. And their sense of dependence is weakened by the conscious power of changing their masters, if they feel themselves offended. Thus comfortably situated at present, what are their prospects in marrying? Without knowledge or capital, either for business, or farming, and unused, and therefore unable to earn a subsistence by daily labour, their only refuge seems to be a miserable alehouse, which certainly offers no very enchanting prospect of a happy evening to their lives. By much the greater part, therefore, deterred by this uninviting view of their future situation, content themselves with remaining single where they are.

If this sketch of the state of society in England be near the truth, and I do not conceive that it is exaggerated, it will be allowed, that the preventive check to population in this country operates, though with varied force, through all the classes of the community. The same observation will hold true with regard to all old states. The effects, indeed, of these restraints upon marriage are but too conspicuous in

37

the consequent vices that are produced in almost every part of the world, vices, that are continually involving both sexes in inextricable unhappiness.

Positive Checks in England

The positive check to population by which I mean the check that represses an increase which is already begun, is confined chiefly, though not perhaps solely, to the lowest orders of society. This check is not so obvious to common view as the other I have mentioned, and, to prove distinctly the force and extent of its operation would require, perhaps, more data than we are in possession of. But I believe it has been very generally remarked by those who have attended to bills of mortality that of the number of children who die annually, much too great a proportion belongs to those who may be supposed unable to give their offspring proper food and attention, exposed as they are occasionally to severe distress and confined, perhaps, to unwholesome habitations and hard labour. This mortality among the children of the poor has been constantly taken notice of in all towns. It certainly does not prevail in an equal degree in the country, but the subject has not hitherto received sufficient attention to enable any one to say that there are not more deaths in proportion among the children of the poor, even in the country, than among those of the middling and higher classes. Indeed, it seems difficult to suppose that a labourer's wife who has six children, and who is sometimes in absolute want of bread, should be able always to give them the food and attention necessary to support life.

> *"Is it necessary for me to give any more details of this vile and infamous doctrine [Malthus's population theory], this repulsive blasphemy against man and nature?"*

Overpopulation Is a Myth

Frederick Engels

The work of Thomas Malthus generated a tremendous reaction, both positive and negative. Frederick Engels (1820–1895) responded to Malthus with as much force as anyone, and his conclusion was that Malthusian theory was very misguided. The following viewpoint is from Engels's *Outline of a Critique of Political Economy*, which was published in 1844. Engels asserts that Malthusian theory confuses means of subsistence with means of employment.

Engels was born in Prussia, the son of a textile manufacturer. Because of his revolutionary activities, he was forced to flee Prussia and settle in England. While in England, Engels wrote many books with Karl Marx, the most famous being *The Communist Manifesto*. Engels managed one of his father's factories in England, earning enough to support himself, Marx, and Marx's family.

As you read, consider the following questions:

1. Engels points out that Malthus's theory blames the poor for surplus population. What problem does Engels have with this?
2. What does Engels have to say about the way Malthus handled the concepts of "means of subsistence" and "means of employment"?
3. What are the author's views on the potential for improvements in food production?

Excerpted from Frederick Engels, "Outlines of a Critique of Political Economy" (1844), translated by Ronald L. Meek in *Marx and Engels on the Population Bomb*. New York: International Publishers, 1954.

Malthus, the originator of [the theory of population], asserts that population constantly exerts pressure on the means of subsistence; that as production is increased, population increases in the same proportion; and that the inherent tendency of population to multiply beyond the available means of subsistence is the cause of all poverty and all vice. For if there are too many people, then in one way or another they must be eliminated; they must die, either by violence or through starvation. When this has happened, however, a gap appears once more, and this is immediately filled by other propagators of population, so that the old poverty begins anew. Moreover, this is the case under all conditions—not only in the civilized but also in the natural state of man. The savages of New Holland, who live *one* to the square mile, suffer just as much from overpopulation as England. In short, if we want to be logical, we have to recognize *that the earth was already overpopulated when only one man existed*. Now the consequence of this theory is that since it is precisely the poor who constitute this surplus population, nothing ought to be done for them, except to make it as easy as possible for them to starve to death; to convince them that this state of affairs cannot be altered and that there is no salvation for their entire class other than that they should propagate as little as possible; or that if this is not practicable, it is at any rate better that a State institution for the painless killing of the children of the poor should be set up—as suggested by "Marcus" [pseudonym of an English author who published in 1858 a pamphlet entitled *On the Possibility of Limiting Populousness*, in which Malthus's theory was carried to an absurdity]—each working-class family being allowed two-and-a-half children, and the excess being painlessly destroyed. The giving of alms would be a crime, since it would encourage the growth of surplus population; but it would be very advantageous to make poverty a crime and the workhouse a corrective institution, as has already happened in England under the new "liberal" Poor Law. It is true, of course, that this theory does not accord at all well with the biblical teaching of the perfection of God and of his creation, but "it is a bad refutation which puts forward the Bible against the facts."

Means of Subsistence vs. Means of Employment

Is it necessary for me to give any more details of this vile and infamous doctrine, this repulsive blasphemy against man and nature, or to follow up its consequences any further? Here, brought before us at last, is the immorality of the economists in its highest form. What were all the wars and horrors of the monopoly system when compared with this theory? And it is precisely this theory which is the cornerstone of the liberal system of free trade, whose fall will bring the whole edifice down with it. For once competition has here been proved to be the cause of misery, poverty and crime, who will still dare to say a word in its defense? . . .

If Malthus had not taken such a one-sided view of the matter, he could not have missed seeing that surplus population or labor power is always bound up with surplus wealth, surplus capital and surplus landed property. Population is too great only when productive power in general is too great. The state of affairs in every overpopulated country, in particular England, from the time when Malthus wrote onwards, demonstrates this quite unmistakably. These were the facts which Malthus ought to have examined in their entirety, and whose examination ought to have led to the correct conclusion; instead, he picked out one of these facts, neglecting the others, and thus arrived at his own crazy conclusion. His second mistake was to confuse means of subsistence with means of employment. That population always presses against the means of employment, that the number of people who are propagated corresponds to the number who can be employed, in short, that the propagation of labor power has up to now been regulated by the law of competition and has therefore also been subject to periodical crises and fluctuations—all these are facts, the establishment of which stands to the credit of Malthus. But means of employment are not means of subsistence. The means of employment increase only as the final result of an increase of machine power and capital; whereas the means of subsistence increase as soon as there is any increase at all in productive power. Here a new contradiction in political economy comes to light. The demand of the economists is not a real demand, their consumption is an artificial consumption. For the economists, only those who can offer an equivalent for what they receive are real demanders, real consumers. If, however, it is a fact that every adult produces more than he can himself consume, that children are like trees, returning abundantly the expenditure laid out on them—and surely these are facts?—one would imagine that every worker ought to be able to produce far more than he needs, and that the community ought therefore to be glad to furnish him with everything that he requires; one would imagine that a large family would be a most desirable gift to the community. But the economists, with their crude outlook, know no other equivalent apart from that which is paid over to them in tangible hard cash. They are so firmly entangled in their contradictions that they are just as little concerned with the most striking facts as they are with the most scientific principles.

A Resolution of Malthus's Contradiction

We shall destroy the contradiction simply by resolving it. With the fusion of those interests which now conflict with one another, there will disappear the antithesis between surplus population in one place and surplus wealth in another, and also the wonderful phenomenon—more wonderful than all the wonders of all the religions put together—that a nation must starve to death from sheer wealth and abundance; and there will disappear too the crazy assertion that the earth does not possess the power to feed mankind. This assertion is the highest wisdom of Christian economics—and that our economics is essentially Christian I could have demonstrated from its every statement, from its every category, and shall in due time so demonstrate. The Malthusian theory is merely the economic expression of the religious dogma of the contradiction between spirit and nature, and of the corruption of both resulting from it. I hope I have shown the futility of this contradiction—which has long been resolved for religion and together with it—in the economic sphere also; moreover, I will not accept any defense of the Malthusian theory as competent which does not begin by explaining to me, on the basis of the theory itself, how a people can die of hunger from sheer abundance, and which does not bring this explanation into harmony with reason and the facts.

Marx on the Laws of Population

The laboring population therefore produces, along with the accumulation of capital produced by it, the means by which itself is made relatively superfluous, is turned into a relative surplus-population; and it does this to an always increasing extent. This is a law of population peculiar to the capitalist mode of production; and in fact every specific historic mode of production has its own special laws of population, historically valid within its limits alone. An abstract law of population exists for plants and animals only, and only insofar as man has not interfered with them.

Karl Marx, *Capital*, vol. 1, 1867.

The Malthusian theory, however, was an absolutely necessary transitional stage, which has taken us infinitely further forward. Thanks to this theory, as also thanks to economics in general, our attention has been drawn to the productive power of the soil and of humanity, so that now, having triumphed over this economic despair, we are forever secure from the fear of overpopulation. From this theory we derive the most powerful economic arguments in favor of a social reorganization; for even if Malthus were altogether right, it would still be necessary to carry out this reorganization immediately, since only this reorganization, only the enlightenment of the masses which it can bring with it, can make possible that moral restraint upon the instinct for reproduction which Malthus himself puts forward as the easiest and most effective countermeasure against overpopulation. Thanks to this theory we have come to recognize in the dependence of man upon competitive conditions his most complete degradation. It has shown us that in the last analysis private property has turned man into a commodity, whose production and consumption also depend only on demand; that the system of competition has thereby slaughtered, and is still slaughtering today, millions of people—all this we have seen, and all this impels us to do away with this degradation of humanity by doing away with private property, competition and conflicting interests.

However, in order to deprive the general fear of overpopulation of all foundation, let us return once again to the question of the relation of productive power to population. Malthus puts forward a calculation upon which his whole system is based. Population increases in geometrical progression—1+2+4+8+16+32, etc. The productive power of the land increases in arithmetical progression—1+2+3+4+5+6. The difference is obvious and horrifying—but is it correct? Where has it been proved that the productivity of the land increases in arithmetical progression? The area of land is limited—that is perfectly true. But the labor power to be employed on this area increases together with the population; and even if we assume that the increase of output associated with this increase of labor is not always proportionate to the latter, there still remains a third element—which the economists, however, never consider as important—namely, science, the progress of which is just as limitless and at least as rapid as that of population. For what great advances is the agriculture of this century obliged to chemistry alone—and indeed to two men alone, Sir Humphry Davy and Justus Liebig? But science increases at least as fast as population; the latter increases in proportion to the size of the previous generation, and science advances in proportion to the body of knowledge passed down to it by the previous generation, that is, in the most normal conditions it also grows in geometrical progression—and what is impossible for science? But it is ridiculous to speak of overpopulation while the valley of the Mississippi alone contains enough waste land to accommodate the whole population of Europe, while altogether only one-third of the earth can be described as cultivated, and while the productivity of this third could be increased sixfold and more merely by applying improvements which are already known.

"*Though it is difficult to be quite certain,
one could expect most people to be able to
live and reproduce in the conditions
considered.*"

Science Will Solve the Population Problem

John H. Fremlin

John H. Fremlin is professor emeritus of applied radioactivity at the University of Birmingham, England. Fremlin's major research emphasis has been on the relative health risks of different energy sources. His book *Power Production: What Are the Risks?* deals with these concerns. In the following viewpoint, originally published in 1964, Fremlin postulates a series of stages in adapting the earth to population growth that would eventually allow the planet to sustain up to 10 quintillion (10^{18}) people.

As you read, consider the following questions:

1. What lifestyle changes would people have to make to accommodate the ever-increasing population densities envisioned in Fremlin's scenario?
2. Why doesn't Fremlin believe that food production for an ever-increasing world population is a problem?
3. What one factor does the author believe could force a limit on the absolute size of the world's population?

Abridged from J.H. Fremlin, "How Many People Can the World Support?" *New Scientist* 415 (1964): 285–87. Reprinted with permission.

The world population is now about 3 billion and is increasing at a rate corresponding to a doubling in 37 years. In view of the increasing importance attached to the immediate effects of the rapid growth in human numbers, it is of interest to examine ultimate technical limits to this growth. Traditionally, these limits have usually been regarded as fixed by possible food supplies although, in practice, at least in historical times, the actual limiting factor has more often been disease.

Diseases are now nearly, and will soon be entirely, eliminated as effective controllers of population growth but it is not at all clear that difficulties in food production will take their place. It is true that there is a limit to the improvement of agricultural output by application of existing scientific knowledge, but by the time this limit is reached other methods of food-production will have been devised. I shall explore the possibility that the real limits are physical rather than biological.

I shall assume throughout an effective degree of world co-operation in the application of food technology, etc. This is quite evidently essential if the maximum world population is to be reached. There are of course many ways of *not* reaching the maximum, but none of these will be discussed here.

In order to give a time scale, it is supposed that the rate of increase of population remains constant at the present value—that is to say, doubling every 37 years. In fact the rate is itself accelerating, so that, in the absence of limitations, this time scale will be too long.

Stage 1: Up to 400 Billion in 260 Years

Using existing crop plants and methods it may not be practicable to produce adequate food for more than four doublings of the world population, though the complete elimination of all land wild-life, the agricultural use of roofs over cities and roads, the elimination of meat-eating and the efficient harvesting of sea food might allow two or three further doublings—say seven in all. That would give us, with the present doubling time of 37 years, 260 years to develop less conventional methods, and would allow the population of the world to increase to about 130 times its present size, or about 400 billion.

46

Stage 2: Up to 3 Trillion in 370 Years

The area of ice-free sea is some three times that of land. Photosynthesis by single-celled marine organisms may be more efficient than that of the best land plants. If organisms could be found capable of the theoretical maximum efficiency (8 percent of total solar radiation, according to A.A. Niciporovic), we should gain a factor of three in yield. We could then double our numbers a further three more times if all the wild-life in the sea, too, was removed and replaced by the most useful organisms growing under controlled conditions, with the optimum concentration of carbonates, nitrates and minerals. (Of course a reserve of specimens of potentially useful species could be preserved, perhaps in a dormant state.) Again, for maximum efficiency we must harvest and consume directly the primary photosynthesising organisms, rather than allow the loss of efficiency involved in the food-chains leading to such secondary organisms as zooplankton or fish.

By this stage, we should have had ten doublings, which at the present rate would take some 370 years, with a final world population of 3 trillion. Since the world's surface (land and sea) is 500 trillion square metres, each person would have a little over 160 square metres for his maintenance—about a thirtieth of an acre—which does not seem unreasonable by more than a factor of two, so long as no important human activity other than food production takes place on the surface.

No serious shortages of important elements need be envisaged so far, though extensive mining operations for phosphates might be needed, and we have not yet approached any real limit.

Stage 3: Up to 15 Trillion in 450 Years

At first sight, it seems that a very big leap forward could be taken if we use sources of power other than sunlight for photosynthesis. The solar power received at the Earth's surface is only about 1 kilowatt per square metre at the equator at midday, and the average value over the day and night sides of the globe is a quarter of this. Over half of it is in the regions of the spectrum of no use for photosynthesis.

About 1 kilowatt-year per square metre could be produced by the complete fission of the uranium and thorium in about 3 cm depth of the Earth's crust or by fusion of the deuterium in about 3 mm depth of seawater, so that adequate power should be available for some time. It is, however, difficult to see how the overall thermal efficiency from fuel to the light actually used for photosynthesis could be even as good as the ratio of useful to non-useful solar radiation (about 40 percent).

Quality vs. Quantity of Life

If we were willing to be crowded together closely enough, to eat foods which would bear little resemblance to the foods we eat today, and to be deprived of simple but satisfying luxuries such as fireplaces, gardens and lawns, a world population of 50 billion persons would not be out of the question. And if we really put our minds to the problem we could construct floating islands where people might live and where algae farms could function, and perhaps 100 billion persons could be provided for. If we set strict limits to physical activities so that caloric requirements could be kept at very low levels, perhaps we could provide for 200 billion persons.

Harrison Brown in Garrett Hardin, ed., *Population, Evolution, and Birth Control: A Collage of Controversial Ideas*, 2nd ed., 1969.

It would, therefore, be better to use large satellite reflectors in orbit to give extra sunlight to the poles and to the night side of the Earth. A large number of mirrors could be maintained in quasi-stable orbits about 1½ million kilometres outside the Earth's orbit, any deviations being controlled by movable "sails" using the pressure of sunlight. To double our total radiation income would require a total area of about 100 million square kilometres of mirror which, in aluminium a tenth of a micron thick, would weigh about 30 million tons. With plenty of people to design and make the equipment it should not be difficult by the time it would be required, and it would bring the whole Earth to equatorial conditions, melting the polar ice and allowing one further doubling of population.

A second doubling of radiation income would give the whole Earth midday equatorial conditions round the clock, which would be exceedingly difficult to cope with without serious overheating. The overall efficiency of local power sources for photosynthesis is likely to be less than that of sunlight, so that no real gain in ultimate population size can be expected from their use, without an even more serious overheating of the entire globe.

If, however, the mirrors outside the Earth's orbit were made of selectively reflecting material, reflecting only the most useful part of the spectrum, and if a further satellite filter were used, inside the Earth's orbit, to deflect the useless 60 percent of direct solar radiation, a further gain of a factor of 2½ should easily be possible without creating thermally impossible conditions, at the cost only of perhaps a 10–100 times increase of weight of mirror plus filter—not difficult for the larger population with an extra 50 years of technical development. We should then have attained a world population of 15 trillion about 450 years from now.

Stage 4: Up to 1 Quadrillion in 680 Years

A considerably larger gain is in principle obtainable if the essential bulk foods: fats, carbohydrates, amino acids and so on, could be directly synthesised. Biological methods might still be permitted for a few special trace compounds. The direct rate of energy production resulting from the conversion of our food into our waste products is only about 100 watts per person and, if high-temperature energy from nuclear fuel (or sunlight) could be efficiently used, waste products could in principle be changed back into food compounds with the absorption of little more energy. Cadavers could be homogenised and would not, at least for physical reasons, need to be chemically treated at all. The fresh mineral material which would have to be processed to allow for population growth would be much less than 1 percent of the turnover, and its energy requirements can be neglected.

If we suppose that the overall efficiency could not be increased beyond 50 percent, a further 100 watts per person would be dissipated as heat in the process of feeding him. We have some hundreds of years to work up the efficiency to this value, so at least this ought to be possible. Some further power would be needed for light, operation of circulation machinery, communications etc., but 50 watts per person should suffice.

As we have seen, the long-term average heat income of the Earth's surface is at present about 250 watts per square metre, and this could be doubled without raising the temperature above the normal equatorial value. (The initial rate of rise would be low till the polar ice had gone, which might take 100 years.) We thus have 500 watts per head, could support 1 quadrillion people altogether. The population density would be 2 per square metre, averaged over the entire land and sea surface of the Earth.

Stage 4a: Up to 12 Quadrillion in 800 Years: Dead End

Above 2 people per square metre, severe refrigeration problems occur. If the oceans were used as a heat sink, their mean temperature would have to rise about 1°C per year to absorb 500 watts per square metre. This would be all right for the doubling time of 37 years, at the end of which we should have 4 people per square metre. Half another doubling time could be gained if efficient heat pumps (which, for reasons of thermal efficiency, would require primary energy sources of very high temperature) could be used to bring the ocean to the boil.

Two more doublings would be permitted if the oceans were converted into steam, though that would create an atmospheric pressure comparable with the mean ocean bottom pressure at present. Since the resulting steam blanket would also be effectively opaque to all radiation, no further heat sink could be organised and this procedure would therefore seem to lead to a dead end.

Stage 5: Up to 60 Quadrillion in 890 Years

A preferable scheme would be the opposite one of roofing in the ocean to stop evaporation (this would, in any case, probably have been done long before, for housing) and hermetically sealing the outer surface of the planet. All of the atmosphere not required for ventilation of the living spaces could then be pumped into compression tanks, for which no great strength would be needed if they were located on ocean bottoms. Heat pumps could then be used to transfer heat to the solid outer skin, from which, in the absence of air, it would be radiated directly into space. The energy radiated from a black body goes up as T^4, where T is the absolute temperature (°K), but for a *fixed rate* of heat extraction from the living space, at a fixed temperature (say, 30°C or 303°K), the heat-power *radiated* must for thermodynamic reasons be proportional to T even if the refrigeration equipment is perfectly efficient (see any good textbook on the principles of refrigeration). Hence the rate of heat extraction will go up no faster than T^3 where T is the outer surface temperature.

Other Possible Limitations

All the same, this gives more promising results than would the use of the ocean as a temporary heat sink. An outer skin temperature of 300°C would give a heat extraction of 3 kW per square metre and 1,000°C would give an extraction ten times greater. If heat removal were the sole limitation, then we could manage about 120 persons per square metre for an outer skin temperature of 1,000°C—which represents nearly six further doublings of population after the end of Stage 4, with a world population of 60 quadrillion in 890 years' time. 1,000°C may be a rather modest figure for the technology of A.D. 2854 and the population could, as far as heat is concerned, be able to double again for each rise of absolute skin temperature of $\sqrt[3]{2}$ or 26 percent. The difficulties in raising it much further while keeping all thermodynamic efficiencies high would, however, seem to be formidable. A rise to 2,000°C would give us less than three further doublings.

We seem, therefore, to have found one possible absolute limit to human population, due to the heat problem, which at the present rate would be reached 800–1,000 years from now, with a world population of 10^{16}–10^{18}. . . .

Other possible limitations than heat will doubtless have occurred to readers, but these do not seem to be absolute. The most obvious is perhaps the housing problem for 120 persons per square metre. We can safely assume, however, that in 900 years' time the construction of continuous 2,000-storey buildings over land and sea alike should be quite easy. That would give 7½ square metres of floor space for each person in 1,000 storeys (though wiring, piping, ducting and lifts [elevators] would take up to half of that) and leave the other 1,000 storeys for the food-producing and refrigerating machinery. It is clear that, even at much lower population densities, very little horizontal circulation of persons, heat or supplies could be tolerated and each area of a few kilometres square, with a population about equal to the present world population, would have to be nearly self-sufficient. Food would all be piped in liquid form and, of course, clothes would be unnecessary.

Raw materials should not be a problem. The whole of the oceans and at least the top 10 kilometres of the Earth's crust would be available, giving a wide choice of building, plumbing and machine-building materials. Even with 8 tons of people per square metre (reckoning 15 people to the ton) all the necessary elements of life could be obtained; some from air and sea (C, H, O, N, Na, Cl, Ca, K and some trace elements) and some from the top 100 metres of solid crust (Fe, S, P, I and remaining trace elements). Only after a further hundredfold increase in population would it be needful to go below the top 10 km of crust for some elements (N, S, P, I). Such an increase would need an outer skin temperature of 5,000°C (comparable with the surface of the Sun) to radiate away the body heat, which would seem to be well beyond the possible limits.

A question of obvious importance which is not easy to answer is whether people could in fact live the nearly sessile [permanently attached to a base] lives, with food and air piped in and wastes piped out, which would be essential. Occasional vertical and random horizontal low speed vehicular or moving-belt travel over a few hundred metres would be permissible, however, so that each individual could choose his friends out of some ten million people, giving adequate social variety, and of course communication by video-phone would be possible with anyone on the planet. One could expect some ten million Shakespeares and rather more Beatles to be alive at any one time, so that a good range of television entertainment should be available. Little heat-producing exercise could be tolerated. The extrapolation from the present life of a car-owning, flat-dwelling office-worker to such an existence might well be less than from that of the neolithic hunter to that of the aforesaid office-worker. Much more should be known about social conditioning in a few hundred years' time and, though it is difficult to be quite certain, one could expect most people to be able to live and reproduce in the conditions considered.

Science Will Not Solve the
Population Problem

Garrett Hardin

Garrett Hardin is professor emeritus of human ecology at
the University of California, Santa Barbara. During the last
three decades, he has been one of the most productive and
influential scholars calling for Zero Population Growth
(births equaling deaths) on planet Earth. In the following
viewpoint, Hardin argues that those who rely on scientific
progress to solve the problems of overpopulation are simply
unwilling to face facts. To illustrate, he projects the costs of
interstellar migration as a solution to overpopulation, and
finds the equations unworkable.

As you read, consider the following questions:
1. How much does Hardin estimate it would cost to send
   one person to a habitable planet 4.3 light-years away?
2. Hardin points out that it would take at least 350 years for
   humans to reach another habitable planet and that births
   would have to equal deaths during this 10-generation
   voyage. What paradoxes does he say that this represents?

Garrett Hardin, "Interstellar Migration and the Population Problem," *Journal of
Heredity* 50 (1959): 68–70. Reprinted by permission of Oxford University Press.

Anyone who discusses population problems with lay audiences is, sooner or later, confronted with questions of this sort: "But why worry about overpopulation? Won't we soon be able to send our surplus population to other planets?" It is not only the audience that adopts this point of view; sometimes the lecturer does, as appears from an Associated Press dispatch of 6 June 1958. Monsignor Irving A. DeBlanc, director of the National Catholic Welfare Conference's Family Life Bureau, is reported as favoring such mass migration, "deploring an often expressed idea that birth control is the only answer to problems created by a fast-growing world population."

Neither physicists nor professional demographers have, so far as I know, recommended extra-terrestrial migration as a solution to the population problem, but the idea appears to be gaining ground among the laity even without scientific support. The psychological reasons for embracing this idea are two. On the one hand, some Roman Catholics welcome it because it appears to offer an escape from the dilemma created by the Church's stand against "artificial" methods of birth control. On the other hand, citizens of all churches worship the new religion called Progress, of which Jules Verne is the prophet. In this religion all things are possible (except acceptance of the impossible). Who is to set limits to Science (with a capital S)? Yesterday, the telephone and the radio; today television and intercontinental ballistic missiles (ICBMs); and tomorrow,—Space!—which will solve all our earthly problems, of course.

This is heady stuff. Strictly speaking, since it springs from an essentially religious feeling and is non-rational, it cannot be answered by a rational argument. Nevertheless, for the sake of those bystanders whose minds are still open to a rational analysis it is worthwhile reviewing the facts and principles involved in the proposal to solve the population problem by interplanetary travel.

The Cost of Space Travel

It now [1959] seems possible that, before the century is out, manned landings may be made on Venus or Mars, with the establishment of temporary quarters thereon. But all evidence points to the unsuitability of these, or any other planets of our sun, as abodes for *Homo sapiens*. We must, therefore, look beyond the solar system, to other stars for possible planets for colonization.

The nearest star is Alpha Centauri, which is 4.3 light-years away. How long would it take us to get there? The rockets that we are now planning to send to the moon will have a maximum velocity in the neighborhood of 10 kilometers per second, or about 19,000 miles per hour. This may sound fast. But a body traveling at such a speed towards Alpha Centauri (which is 4.07×10^{13} kilometers distant) would require 129,000 years to reach its destination. Surely no one believes that a fleet of spaceships with so long a transit time would solve our explosive population problem. The question is, then, what is the probability of improvements in space travel that would significantly cut down the time required to make such an interstellar journey? In trying to answer this question I have relied on an analysis by L.R. Shepherd [in L.J. Carter, ed., *Realities of Space Travel*, 1957], to which the interested reader is referred for technical details.

Shepherd presumes a technology in the release and utilization of nuclear energy that may take several centuries to achieve. To give the worshippers of Progress the maximum advantage we will assume that such an advanced technology is available *now*, and see how long it would take to travel to the nearest star. Using fantastically optimistic assumptions, Shepherd calculates that it might be possible to make the transit in a mere 350 years. The average speed of the trip would be about 7,000,000 m.p.h., though the maximum speed would be somewhat more, since 50 years would be required for acceleration at the beginning of the trip and another 50 years for deceleration at the end. (In passing, it should be noted that acceleration is more of a limiting factor than is velocity.)

The Economics of Interstellar Migration

To evaluate interstellar migration as a population control measure we must examine its economics. Here the unknowns are obviously great, but from data assembled by A.V. Cleaver [also in Carter, *Realities of Space Travel*] it appears that the foreseeable cost of a rocket ship could hardly be as little as $50 a pound, assuming economies of mass production and allowing nothing for research and development costs. How many pounds of ship would be required per man? Since we have no data on such a spaceship, let us borrow from our knowledge of atomic submarines, which are perhaps not too dissimilar. A spaceship designed to be self-maintaining for 350 years could hardly be less complicated or less bulky than an underwater craft capable of operating away from its depots for only a month or two. According to a news release the submarine *Seawolf* weighs 3,000 tons and carries 100 men, a burden of 60,000 lbs. per man. A spaceship of a similar design, at $50 a pound, would cost $3,000,000 per man travelling in it. Would this be a reasonable cost for solving the population problem? Those who propose such a solution presume, or even recommend, that we do not alter our present reproductive habits. What would it cost to keep the population of the United States fixed at its present level by shipping off the surplus in spaceships?

According to a recent estimate of the U.S. Bureau of the Census our population is increasing by about 3,000,000 people per year. To ship this increase off to other planets would, on the above conservative assumptions, cost about $9 trillion per year. The Gross National Product is now nearly $450 billion per year. In other words, to solve our national population problem by this means we would, then, have to spend 20 times as much as our entire income on this purpose alone, allowing nothing for any other use, not even for food. It would surely be unrealistic to suppose that we shall do this in the near future.

Another aspect of the population problem is worth commenting on. Many philanthropically minded citizens feel that it is an obligation of the United States to solve the population problems of the entire world, believing that we should use the riches produced by our technology to make up for the deficiencies in luck or foresight of other peoples. Let's examine the economics of so doing. According to a recent estimate the population of the world is increasing at a rate of 123,000 per day. To remove one day's increment by the postulated spaceship would cost about $369 billion. In other words, we Americans, by cutting our standard of living down to 18 percent of its present level, could in *one year's time* set aside enough capital to finance the exportation of *one day's increase* in the population of the entire world. Such a philanthropic desire to share the wealth may be judged noble in intent, but hardly in effect.

". . . An Atmosphere That Could Support Life . . ."

From *Herblock on All Fronts* (New American Library, 1980). Reprinted with permission.

In passing, it should be noted that we have so far made no mention of certain assumptions that are of critical importance in the whole picture. We have assumed that our nearest star has planets; that at least one of these planets is suitable for human habitation; that this suitable planet is uninhabited—or, if inhabited, that the humanoids thereon will gracefully commit suicide when they find we need their planet for our *Lebensraum* [term used esp. by Nazis to denote territory required for political and economic expansion]. (The tender feelings that would make impossible the control of reproduction on earth would presumably not interfere with the destruction of life on other planets.) Should Alpha Centauri have no planet available for migratory earthlings, our expedition would presumably set out for an even more distant star, perhaps eventually becoming a latterday interstellar Flying Dutchman.

Paradoxes of Space Emigration

Cogent as the economic analysis of the problem is, it does not touch on issues that are of even greater importance. Consider the human situation on board this astronautical *Mayflower*. For 350 years the population would have to live under conditions of complete sociological stasis, the like of which has never been known before. No births would be permitted, except to replace the dead (whose substance would, of course, have to be returned to the common stores). Marriages would certainly have to be controlled, as would all other social interactions, and with an iron hand. In the spaceship, Progress would be unendurable. The social organization would have to persist unchanged for 10 generations' time, otherwise there would be the risk that some of the descendants of the original crew might wish to change the plans. It would be as though the spaceship had to set sail, so to speak, under Captain John Smith and arrive at its goal under President Eisenhower, without the slightest change in ideas or ideals. Can we who have so recently seen how fragile and mutable a flower Education is suppose that we could set up so stable a system of indoctrination? Paradoxically, only a people who worship Progress would propose to launch such a craft, but such worshippers would be the worst possible passengers for it.

Those who seriously propose interstellar migration as a solution to overpopulation do so because they are unwilling to accept the necessity of consciously controlling population numbers by means already at hand. They are unwilling to live, or to admit living, in a closed universe. Yet—and here is the second paradox—that is precisely the sort of universe the interstellar migrants would be confined to, for some 10 generations. Since the present annual rate of growth of the world's population is about 1.7 percent, by the time the first ship arrived at its destination, the whole fleet of spaceships en route would enclose a total population six times as large as that still present on the earth. That is, in attempting to escape the necessities of living in a closed universe, we would confine to the closed universes of spaceships a population six times as great as that of the earth.

Moreover, there would be a differential element in the emigration from the mother planet. The proposal to emigrate is made by those who, for religious or other reasons, are unwilling to curb the reproductive proclivities of mankind. But not for such as these is the kingdom of a spaceship. They must stay behind while the ship is manned by those whose temperament creates no need for emigration. The reproductively prudent would be exiled from a world made unbearably crowded by the imprudent—who would stay home to perpetuate the problem into the next generation. Whether the difference between the two groups is basically biological, or merely sociological, would not matter. In either case, natural selection would enter in. The end result of this selective emigration would be to create an earth peopled only by men and women unwilling to control their breeding, and unwilling, therefore, to make use of the very means they propose to escape the consequences.

A Return to the Vision of Malthus

The proposal to eliminate overpopulation by resort to interstellar migration is thus seen to yield not a rational solution at all. The proposal is favored only by men who have more faith in gadgetry than they do in rationality. Should men of this temper prevail, and should the gadgetry prove equal to the quantitative demands put upon it, the result would nevertheless be the ultimate production of a world in which the only remaining controls of population would be the "misery and vice" foreseen by Malthus 161 years ago.

Periodical Bibliography

The following articles have been selected to supplement the diverse views presented in this chapter. Addresses are provided for periodicals not indexed in the *Readers' Guide to Periodical Literature*, the *Alternative Press Index*, the *Social Sciences Index*, or the *Index to Legal Periodicals and Books*.

Giovanni Botero
"Giovanni Botero on the Forces Governing Population," *Population and Development Review*, vol. 11, no. 2, 1985.

R. Cantillon
"Cantillon on Tastes and Population," *Population and Development Review*, vol. 10, no. 4, 1984.

Denis Diderot
"Diderot's Encyclopedia on Population," *Population and Development Review*, vol. 15, no. 1, 1989.

E. Dupreel
"Dupreel on Population and Progress," *Population and Development Review*, vol. 8, no. 4, 1982.

Benjamin Franklin
"Benjamin Franklin on the Causes and Consequences of Population Growth," *Population and Development Review*, vol. 11, no. 1, 1985.

Henry George
"Henry George on Disproof of the Malthusian Theory," *Population and Development Review*, vol. 13, no. 2, 1987.

Francis Hutcheson
"Francis Hutcheson on the Rights of Society," *Population and Development Review*, vol. 24, no. 4, 1998.

Thomas Jefferson
"Thomas Jefferson on Population," *Population and Development Review*, vol. 19, no. 1, 1993.

Frank Notestein
"Frank Notestein on Population Growth and Economic Development," *Population and Development Review*, vol. 9, no. 2, 1983.

E.G. Ravenstein
"Ravenstein on Global Carrying Capacity," *Population and Development Review*, vol. 16, no. 1, 1990.

Alfred Sauvy
"Alfred Sauvy on the World Population Problem: A View in 1949," *Population and Development Review*, vol. 16, no. 4, 1990.

Leonard Sismondi
"Sismondi on Population," *Population and Development Review*, vol. 16, no. 3, 1990.

Sir James Steuart
"Sir James Steuart on the Causes of Human Multiplication," *Population and Development Review*, vol. 24, no. 1, 1998.

How Will Population Grow in the Twenty-First Century?

Chapter Preface

It is relatively easy for demographers who study population to look back and recount how population has grown in the past. There is little to no debate about whether the species *Homo sapiens* has been growing on the planet Earth, and that most of that growth has taken place in an extremely short period of time, in terms of overall human history. It took over a millennium for human population to grow from less than 400 million at the time of Christ to 1 billion at the beginning of the nineteenth century. It took over another century for the global population to reach 2 billion in 1930. It then took only thirty years for the population to reach 3 billion in 1960, fifteen more years to get to 4 billion in 1975, and another twelve years before the 5 billion mark in 1987. On October 12, 1999, the United Nations Population Division announced that world population had reached 6 billion.

While it is relatively easy to look back and see how population has grown, it is a bit trickier to determine what the future will hold. What can we expect in the not-so-distant future with respect to population growth? Will the "population explosion" continue unabated, to 8, 9, or 10 billion, as the United Nations Population Division predicts? Or will there be, as many demographers suspect, a "birth dearth," in which people all over the world begin having fewer babies? In fact, both these scenarios are possible, as population increases and decreases in different parts of the globe and decreasing fertility rates are offset by increased life expectancies. The authors in the following chapter debate these and other factors that could contribute to overpopulation and underpopulation in the twenty-first century.

> "Most middle-of-the-road demographic projections for the year 2040—less than two generations from now—are in the 8 to 9 billion range."

Global Population Will Reach Crisis Proportions by 2050

J. Kenneth Smail

J. Kenneth Smail is professor of anthropology at Kenyon College and has written numerous articles dealing with human population size and growth. In the following viewpoint, he lists ten reasons, which he terms "inescapable realities" about population growth, to support his conviction that population will increase dramatically in the first half of the twenty-first century. The effects of population growth, he contends, will have disastrous effects on the environment and on all people's quality of life.

As you read, consider the following questions:
1. According to Smail, by how many people per day is the human population increasing?
2. What percentage of the world's population has an adequate standard of living, in the author's view?
3. What three basic factors do demographers multiply together to determine the impact of the human population on the global environment?

Excerpted from "Beyond Population Stabilization: The Case for Dramatically Reducing Global Human Numbers," by J. Kenneth Smail, *Politics and Life Sciences*, September 1997. Reprinted with permission from the author.

The main point of this essay is simply stated. Within the next half-century, it will be essential for the human species to have in place a fully operational, flexibly designed, essentially voluntary, broadly equitable, and internationally coordinated set of initiatives focused on dramatically reducing the then-current world population by at least two-thirds to three-fourths. Given that even with the best of intentions it will take considerable time, unusual patience, exceptional administrative talent, and consummate diplomatic skill to develop and implement such an undertaking (probably on the order of 25 to 50 years), it is important that this process of voluntary consensus building—local, national, and global—begin now.

The mathematical inevitability that human numbers will continue their dramatic increase over the next two generations (to perhaps 9 billion or more by the year 2050), the high probability that this numerical increase will exacerbate still further the systemic problems that already plague humanity (economic, political, environmental, social, moral, etc.), and the growing realization that the Earth's long-term carrying capacity may only be sufficient to sustain a global human population in the 2 to 3 billion range (at an "adequate to comfortable" standard of living) only reinforces this sense of urgency.

There are, however, hopeful signs. In recent years, we have finally begun to come to terms with the fact that the consequences of the twentieth century's rapid and seemingly uncontrolled population growth will soon place us—if it has not done so already—in the midst of the greatest crisis our species has yet encountered.

In order better to appreciate the scope and ramifications of this still partly hidden crisis, I shall briefly call attention to ten essential, incontrovertible, and inescapable realities that must not only be fully understood but soon confronted. . . .

The Exponential Nature of Population Growth

First, during the [twentieth] century world population will have grown from somewhere around 1.6 billion in 1900 to slightly more than 6 billion by the year 2000, an almost four-fold increase in but 100 years. This is an unprecedented numerical expansion. Throughout human history, world population growth measured over similar 100-year intervals has been virtually nonexistent or, at most, modestly incremental; it has only become markedly exponential within the last few hundred years. To illustrate this on a more easily comprehensible scale, based on the present rate of increase of nearly 90 million per year, human population growth during the 1990s alone will amount to nearly one billion, an astonishing 20% increase in but little more than a single decade. Just by itself, this 10 to 11 year increase is equivalent to the total global population in the year 1800 (barely 200 years ago) and is approximately triple the estimated world population (ca. 300 million) at the height of the Roman Empire. It is a chastening thought that even moderate to conservative demographic projections suggest that this billion-per-decade rate of increase will continue well into the [twenty-first] century, and that the current global total of 6.0 billion (late 1999 estimate) could easily reach 9 to 10 billion by mid-twenty-first century.

Second, even if a fully effective program of zero population growth (ZPG) were to be implemented immediately, by limiting human fertility to what demographers term the *replacement rate* (roughly 2.1 children per female), global population would nevertheless continue its rapid rate of expansion. In fact, demographers estimate that it would take at least two to three generations (50 to 75 years) at ZPG fertility levels just to reach a point of population stability, unfortunately at numbers considerably higher than at present. This powerful *population momentum* results from the fact that an unusually high proportion (nearly one-third) of the current world population is under the age of 15 and has not yet reproduced. Even more broad-based population profiles may be found throughout the developing world, where the under-15 age cohort often exceeds 40% and where birth rates have remained high even as mortality rates have fallen. While there are some recent indications that fertility rates are beginning to decline, the current composite for the less-developed world—excluding China—is still nearly double (ca. 3.8) that needed for ZPG.

Third, in addition to fertility levels, it is essential to understand that population growth is also significantly affected by changes in mortality rates. In fact, demographic transition theory suggests that the earlier stages of rapid population expansion are typically fueled more by significant reductions in death rates (i.e., decreased childhood mortality and/or enhanced adult longevity) than by changes in birth rates. Nor does recent empirical data suggest that average human life expectancy has reached anywhere near its theoretical upper limit, in either the developing or developed worlds. Consequently, unless there appears a deadly pandemic, a devastating world war or a massive breakdown in public health (or a combination of all three), it is obvious that ongoing global gains in human longevity will continue to make a major contribution to world population expansion over the next half-century, regardless of whatever progress might be made in reducing fertility.

Six Billion and Counting

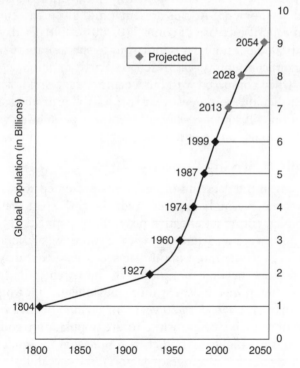

Source: United Nations Population Division, 1999.

A further consequence of this continuing trend is the fact that most national populations will inevitably get "older," with mean ages in the 35 to 40 range and perhaps as many as one-fourth of their members over age 60, as both mortality and fertility rates decline and human numbers (hopefully) reach stable levels. Not surprisingly, each of these aging populations will develop its own unique set of problems to resolve, not the least of which might be understandable but almost certainly misguided efforts to increase the size—and overall economic productivity—of younger age cohorts by encouraging higher fertility.

Fourth, it is important to recognize that the quantitative scale, geographic scope, escalating pace, and functional interconnectedness of these impending demographic changes are of such a magnitude that there are few if any historical precedents to guide us. All previous examples of significant human population expansion—and subsequent (occasionally rapid) decline—have been primarily local or, at most, regional phenomena. At the present time, given the current global rate of increase of some 230,000 people per day (almost 10,000 per hour), it is ludicrous to speak of there being any significant empty spaces left on Earth to colonize, certainly when compared with but a century ago. And it is even more ridiculous to suggest that "off Earth" (extraterrestrial) migration will somehow be sufficient to siphon away excess human population, in either the near or more distant future.

A Finite Carrying Capacity

Fifth, given the data and observations presented thus far, it becomes increasingly apparent that the time span available for implementing an effective program of population "control" may be quite limited, with a window of opportunity—even in the more optimistic scenarios—that may not extend much beyond the middle of the [twenty-first] century. Other projections are more pessimistic, allowing no more than another 15 to 20 years for taking effective remedial action. In any event, while future population trends are notoriously difficult to predict with precision (dependent as they are on a broad range of factors), most middle-of-the-road demographic projections for the year 2040—less than two generations from now—are in the 8 to 9 billion range. . . . By any reasonable standard of comparison, this is hardly the remote future. . . . It is primarily *those already born*—ourselves, our children, and our grandchildren—who will have to confront the overwhelming impact of an additional 3 to 4 billion people within the next 40 to 50 years.

Sixth, it is extremely important to come to terms with the fact that the Earth's long-term carrying capacity, in terms of resources (broadly defined), is indeed finite, despite the continuing use of economic models predicated on seemingly unlimited growth, and notwithstanding the high probability of continued scientific/technological progress. Some further terminological clarification may be useful. "Long-term" is most reasonably defined on the order of several hundred years, at least; it emphatically does not mean the 5 to 15 year horizon typical of much economic forecasting or political prognostication. Over this much longer time span, it thus becomes much more appropriate—perhaps even essential to civilizational survival—to define a sustainable human population size in terms of optimums rather than maximums. In other words, *what "could" be supported in the short term is not necessarily what "should" be humanity's goal over the longer term.*

As far as resources are concerned, whether these be characterized as renewable or nonrenewable, it is becoming increasingly apparent that the era of inexpensive energy (derived from fossil fuels), adequate food supplies (whether plant or animal), readily available or easily extractable raw materials (from wood to minerals), plentiful fresh water, and readily accessible "open space" is rapidly coming to a close, almost certainly within the next half century. And finally, the consequences of future scientific/technological advances—whether in terms of energy production, technological efficiency, agricultural productivity, or creation of alternative materials—are much more likely to be incremental than revolutionary, notwithstanding frequent and grandiose claims for the latter.

Seventh, it is becoming increasingly apparent that rhetoric about "sustainable growth" is at best a continuing exercise in economic self-deception and at worst a politically pernicious oxymoron. Almost certainly, working toward some sort of *steady-state sustainability* is much more realistic scientifically, (probably) more attainable economically, and (perhaps) more prudent politically. Assertions that the Earth might be able to support a population of 10, 15, or even 20 billion people for an indefinite period of time at a standard of living superior to the present are not only cruelly misleading but almost certainly false. Rather, extrapolations from the work of a growing number of ecologists, demographers, and numerous others suggest the distinct possibility that *the Earth's true carrying capacity*—defined simply as humans in long-term adaptive balance with their ecological setting, resource base, and each other—*may already have been exceeded by a factor of two or more.*

To the best of my knowledge, there is no clear-cut or well-documented evidence that effectively contradicts this sobering—perhaps even frightening—assessment. Consequently, since at some point in the not-too-distant future the negative consequences and ecological damage stemming from the mutually reinforcing effects of excessive human reproduction and overconsumption of resources could well become irreversible, and because there is only one Earth with which to experiment, it is undoubtedly better for our species to err on the side of prudence, exercising wherever possible a cautious and careful stewardship.

Impacts on Quality of Life

Eighth, only about 20% of the current world population (ca. 1.2 billion people) could be said to have a *generally adequate* standard of living, defined here as a level of affluence roughly approximating that of the so-called "developed" world (Western Europe, Japan, and North America). The other 80% (ca. 4.8 billion), incorporating most of the inhabitants of what have been termed the "developing nations," live in conditions ranging from mild deprivation to severe deficiency. Despite well-intentioned efforts to the contrary, there is little evidence that this imbalance is going to decrease in any significant way, and a strong likelihood that it may get worse, particularly in view of the fact that more than 90% of all future population expansion is projected to occur in these less-developed regions of the world. In fact, there is growing concern that when this burgeoning population growth in the developing world is combined with excessive or wasteful per capita energy and resource consumption in much of the developed world, widespread environmental deterioration (systemic breakdown?) in a number of the Earth's more heavily stressed ecosystems will become increasingly likely. This is especially worrisome in regions already beset by short-sighted or counterproductive economic policies, chronic political instability, and growing social unrest, particularly when one considers that nearly all nations in the less-developed world currently have an understandable desire—not surprisingly expressed as a fundamental right—to increase their standard of living (per capita energy and resource consumption) to something approximating "first world" levels.

Ninth, to follow up on the point just made, the total impact of human numbers on the global environment is often described as the product of three basic multipliers: (1) population size; (2) per capita energy and resource consumption (affluence); and (3) technological efficiency in the production, utilization, and conservation of such energy and resources. This relationship is usually expressed by some variant of the now well-known I = PAT equation: Impact = Population × Affluence × Technology. This simple formula enables one to demonstrate much more clearly the quantitative scope of humanity's dilemma over the next 50 to 75 years, particularly if the following projections are anywhere near accurate:

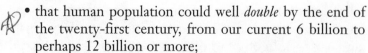

- that human population could well *double* by the end of the twenty-first century, from our current 6 billion to perhaps 12 billion or more;
- that global energy and resource consumption could easily *quadruple* or more during the same period, particularly if (as just indicated in item 8) the less-developed nations are successful in their current efforts to significantly improve their citizens' standard of living to something approaching developed-world norms; and
- that "new technologies" applied to current energy and resource inefficiencies might be successful in reducing per capita waste or effluence *by half*, or even *two-thirds*, in both the developed and developing worlds.

Given these more-or-less realistic estimates, the conclusion seems inescapable that the human species' "total impact" on the Earth's already stressed ecosystem(s) could easily *triple to quadruple* by the middle of the [twenty-first] century. This impact could be even greater if current (and future) efforts at energy and resource conservation turn out to be less successful than hoped for, or if (as seems likely) the mathematical relationship between these several multipliers is something more than simply linear. It is therefore very important to keep a close watch—for harbingers of future trends and/or problems—on current events in the growing group of nations now experiencing rapid economic development and modernization, with particular attention being given to ongoing changes in India and China, two states whose combined size represents nearly half the population of the less-developed world.

Final Considerations

Tenth, and finally, there are two additional considerations—matters not usually factored into the I = PAT equation—that must also be taken into account in any attempt to coordinate appropriate responses to the rapidly increasing global environmental impact described in points 6 through 9 above. First, given current and likely ongoing scientific uncertainties about environmental limits and ecosystem resilience, not to mention the potential dangers of irreversible damage if such limits are stretched too far (i.e., a permanently reduced carrying capacity), it is extremely important to design into any future planning an adequate safety factor (or sufficient margin for error). In other words, any attempt at "guided social engineering" on the massive scale that will clearly be necessary over the next century will require at least as much attention to safety margins, internal coordination, and systems redundancy as may be found in other major engineering accomplishments—from designing airplanes to building the Channel Tunnel to landing astronauts on the moon.

In addition, such planning must consider yet another seemingly intractable problem. Because the human species not only shares the Earth—but has also co-evolved—with literally millions of other life forms, the closely related issues of wilderness conservation and biodiversity preservation must also be taken fully into account, on several different levels (pragmatic, aesthetic, and moral). In simplest terms, it has now become a matter of critical importance to ask some very basic questions about what proportion of the Earth's surface the human species has the right to exploit or transform—or, conversely, how much of the Earth's surface should be reserved for the protection and preservation of all other life forms. As many have argued, often in eloquent terms, our species will likely be more successful in confronting and resolving these questions—not to mention the other complex problems that are now crowding in upon us—if we can collectively come to regard ourselves more as the Earth's long-term stewards than its absolute masters.

To sum up, if the above "inescapable realities" are indeed valid, it is obvious that rational, equitable, and attainable population goals will have to be established in the very near future. It is also obvious that these goals will have to address—and in some fashion resolve—a powerful internal conflict: how to create and sustain an adequate standard of living for *all* the world's peoples, minimizing as much as possible the growing inequities between rich and poor, while simultaneously neither overstressing nor exceeding the Earth's longer-term carrying capacity. *I submit that these goals cannot be reached, or this conflict resolved, unless and until world population is dramatically reduced—to somewhere around two to three billion people—within the next two centuries.*

> *"The evidence now indicates that within*
> *fifty years or so world population will peak*
> *at about eight billion before starting a*
> *fairly rapid decline."*

Global Population Will Decrease After 2050

Max Singer

In the following viewpoint, Max Singer rejects the idea that human population growth is skyrocketing uncontrollably. He maintains that human fertility rates are actually decreasing and that, because people throughout the world are having fewer and fewer children, global population will begin to substantially decrease by the middle of the twenty-first century. However, he warns, this does not mean that population will ever stabilize at a certain level; rather, human populations tend to either increase or decrease, and depend most heavily on people's personal choices about how many children to have. Singer is the founder of the Hudson Institute, a public policy think tank, and coauthor of *The Real World Order*.

As you read, consider the following questions:

1. For how long have U.S. fertility rates been falling, according to the author?
2. What percentage of the world's population does Singer say live in countries that have below-replacement fertility rates?
3. According to Singer, by how much has world fertility dropped in the twentieth century?

Excerpted from "The Population Surprise," by Max Singer, *The Atlantic Monthly*, August 1999. Reprinted with permission from the author.

Fifty years from now the world's population will be declining, with no end in sight. Unless people's values change greatly, several centuries from now there could be fewer people living in the entire world than live in the United States today. The big surprise of the past twenty years is that in not one country did fertility stop falling when it reached the replacement rate—2.1 children per woman. In Italy, for example, the rate has fallen to 1.2. In Western Europe as a whole and in Japan it is down to 1.5. The evidence now indicates that within fifty years or so world population will peak at about eight billion before starting a fairly rapid decline.

Population Will Not Increase Indefinitely, but Neither Will It Stabilize

Because in the past two centuries world population has increased from one billion to nearly six billion, many people still fear that it will keep "exploding" until there are too many people for the earth to support. But that is like fearing that your baby will grow to 1,000 pounds because its weight doubles three times in its first seven years. World population was growing by two percent a year in the 1960s; the rate is now down to one percent a year, and if the patterns of the past century don't change radically, it will head into negative numbers. This view is coming to be widely accepted among population experts, even as the public continues to focus on the threat of uncontrolled population growth.

As long ago as September of 1974 *Scientific American* published a special issue on population that described what demographers had begun calling the "demographic transition" from traditional high rates of birth and death to the low ones of modern society. The experts believed that birth and death rates would be more or less equal in the future, as they had been in the past, keeping total population stable after a level of 10–12 billion people was reached during the transition.

Developments over the past twenty years show that the experts were right in thinking that population won't keep going up forever. They were wrong in thinking that after it stops going up, it will stay level. The experts' assumption that population would stabilize because birth rates would stop falling once they matched the new low death rates has not been borne out by experience. Evidence from more than fifty countries demonstrates what should be unsurprising: in a modern society the death rate doesn't determine the birth rate. If in the long run birth rates worldwide do not conveniently match death rates, then population must either rise or fall, depending on whether birth or death rates are higher. Which can we expect?

Fertility Rates Are Falling Worldwide

The rapid increase in population during the past two centuries has been the result of lower death rates, which have produced an increase in worldwide life expectancy from about thirty to about sixty-two. (Since the maximum—if we do not change fundamental human physiology—is about eighty-five, the world has already gone three fifths as far as it can in increasing life expectancy.) For a while the result was a young population with more mothers in each generation, and fewer deaths than births. But even during this population explosion the average number of children born to each woman—the fertility rate—has been falling in modernizing societies. The prediction that world population will soon begin to decline is based on almost universal human behavior. In the United States fertility has been falling for 200 years (except for the blip of the Baby Boom), but partly because of immigration it has stayed only slightly below replacement level for twenty-five years.

Obviously, if for many generations the birth rate averages fewer than 2.1 children per woman, population must eventually stop growing. Recently the United Nations Population Division estimated that 44 percent of the world's people live in countries where the fertility rate has already fallen below the replacement rate, and fertility is falling fast almost everywhere else. In Sweden and Italy fertility has been below replacement level for so long that the population has become old enough to have more deaths than births. Declines in fertility will eventually increase the average age in the world, and will cause a decline in world population forty to fifty years from now.

Because in a modern society the death rate and the fertility rate are largely independent of each other, world population need not be stable. World population can be stable only if fertility rates around the world average out to 2.1 children per woman. But why should they average 2.1, rather than 2.4, or 1.8, or some other number? If there is nothing to keep each country exactly at 2.1, then there is nothing to ensure that the overall average will be exactly 2.1.

The point is that the number of children born depends on families' choices about how many children they want to raise. And when a family is deciding whether to have another child, it is usually thinking about things other than the national or the world population. Who would know or care if world population were to drop from, say, 5.85 billion to 5.81 billion? Population change is too slow and remote for people to feel in their lives—even if the total population were to double or halve in only a century (as a mere 0.7 percent increase or decrease each year would do). Whether world population is increasing or decreasing doesn't necessarily affect the decisions that determine whether it will increase or decrease in the future. As the systems people would say, there is no feedback loop.

Modern Societies Have Below-Replacement Birth Rates

What does affect fertility is modernity. In almost every country where people have moved from traditional ways of life to modern ones, they are choosing to have too few children to replace themselves. This is true in Western and in Eastern countries, in Catholic and in secular societies. And it is true in the richest parts of the richest countries. The only exceptions seem to be some small religious communities. We can't be sure what will happen in Muslim countries, because few of them have become modern yet, but so far it looks as if their fertility rates will respond to modernity as others' have.

Nobody can say whether world population will ever dwindle to very low numbers; that depends on what values people hold in the future. After the approaching peak, as long as people continue to prefer saving effort and money by having fewer children, population will continue to decline. (This does not imply that the decision to have fewer children is selfish; it may, for example, be motivated by a desire to do more for each child.)

Some people may have values significantly different from those of the rest of the world, and therefore different fertility rates. If such people live in a particular country or population group, their values can produce marked changes in the size of that country or group, even as world population changes only slowly. For example, the U.S. population, be-

The Rapid Drop in Fertility Rates

From 1950 to 1955, the global "total fertility rate" (roughly speaking, the average number of children born per woman per lifetime) was five. That was explosively above the so-called replacement rate of 2.1 children, the level needed to keep a population from falling over time, absent immigration. This scary growth continued for about 15 years until, by 1975 to 1980, fertility had fallen to four children per woman. Fifteen years after that, the rate had fallen to just below three. Today the total fertility rate is estimated at 2.8, and sinking. . . .

But what about women in those teeming less-developed countries (L.D.C.'s)—those swarming places where the population bomb was allegedly ticking most loudly? Even there, the fuse is sputtering. The L.D.C. fertility rate in 1965 to 1970 was six children per woman. Now it's three, and falling more quickly than ever before in demographic history.

Those are broad numbers. Consider some specific nations. Italy, a Catholic country, has a fertility rate of 1.2 children per woman, the world's lowest rate—and the lowest national rate ever recorded (absent famines, plagues, wars or economic catastrophes). India's fertility rate is lower than American rates in the 1950's. The rate in Bangladesh has fallen from 6.2 to 3.4—in just 10 years.

European birthrates of the 1980's, already at record-breaking lows, fell another 20 percent in the 90's, to about 1.4 children per woman. . . . By the year 2060, when its population levels off, Europe will have lost 24 percent of its people. Japanese and Russian rates are also at about 1.4 children. . . .

In the United States, birthrates have been below replacement for 25 straight years. There was an uptick in the late 1980's, but rates have fallen for five of the last six years.

Ben J. Wattenberg, "The Population Explosion Is Over," *New York Times*, November 23, 1997.

cause of immigration and a fertility rate that is only slightly below replacement level, is likely to grow from 4.5 percent of the world today to 10 percent of a smaller world over the next two or three centuries. Much bigger changes in share are possible for smaller groups if they can maintain their difference from the average for a long period of time. (To illustrate: Korea's population could grow from one percent of the world to 10 percent in a single lifetime if it were to increase by two percent a year while the rest of the world population declined by one percent a year.)

People's Values Determine Their Fertility Rates

World population won't stop declining until human values change. But human values may well change—values, not biological imperatives, are the unfathomable variable in population predictions. It is quite possible that in a century or two or three, when just about the whole world is at least as modern as Western Europe is today, people will start to value children more highly than they do now in modern societies. If they do, and fertility rates start to climb, fertility is no more likely to stop climbing at an average rate of 2.1 children per woman than it was to stop falling at 2.1 on the way down.

In only the past twenty years or so world fertility has dropped by 1.5 births per woman. Such a degree of change, were it to occur again, would be enough to turn a long-term increase in world population of one percent a year into a long-term decrease of one percent a year. Presumably fertility could someday increase just as quickly as it has declined in recent decades, although such a rapid change will be less likely once the world has completed the transition to modernity. If fertility rises only to 2.8, just 33 percent over the replacement rate, world population will eventually grow by one percent a year again—doubling in seventy years and multiplying by twenty in only three centuries.

The decline in fertility that began in some countries, including the United States, in the past century is taking a long time to reduce world population because when it started, fertility was very much higher than replacement level. In addition, because a preference for fewer children is associated with modern societies, in which high living standards make time valuable and children financially unproductive and expensive to care for and educate, the trend toward lower fertility couldn't spread throughout the world until economic development had spread. But once the whole world has become modern, with fertility everywhere in the neighborhood of replacement level, new social values might spread worldwide in a few decades. Fashions in families might keep changing, so that world fertility bounced above and below replacement rate. If each bounce took only a few decades or generations, world population would stay within a reasonably narrow range—although probably with a long-term trend in one direction or the other.

The values that influence decisions about having children seem, however, to change slowly and to be very widespread. If the average fertility rate were to take a long time to move from well below to well above replacement rate and back again, trends in world population could go a long way before they reversed themselves. The result would be big swings in world population—perhaps down to one or two billion and then up to 20 or 40 billion.

Whether population swings are short and narrow or long and wide, the average level of world population after several cycles will probably have either an upward or a downward trend overall. Just as averaging across the globe need not result in exactly 2.1 children per woman, averaging across the centuries need not result in zero growth rather than a slowly increasing or slowly decreasing world population. But the long-term trend is less important than the effects of the peaks and troughs. The troughs could be so low that human beings become scarcer than they were in ancient times. The peaks might cause harm from some kinds of shortages.

One implication is that not even very large losses from disease or war can affect the world population in the long run nearly as much as changes in human values do. What we have learned from the dramatic changes of the past few centuries is that regardless of the size of the world population at any time, people's personal decisions about how many children they want can make the world population go anywhere—to zero or to 100 billion or more.

"When more . . . of the world's most highly
industrialized and economically productive
nations do not replenish their numbers,
their role as engines of global growth . . . is
thrown into doubt."

Developed Nations Will Face Severe Underpopulation

Barbara Crossette

In the following viewpoint, *New York Times* writer Barbara Crossette, reporting on the UN population conference in New York in November 1997, describes the concern that many demographers have expressed over the declining fertility rates in the United States, Japan, and many European countries. Decreased fertility may adversely affect these nations' economic productivity, she writes. Developed nations will also face massive immigration from developing nations, which have higher fertility rates and poorer economies. Some industrialized countries are providing incentives for couples to reproduce, she notes, but demographers estimate that almost half the world's nations will have below-replacement fertility rates by 2015.

As you read, consider the following questions:

1. Why is the U.S. population growing more rapidly than other developed nations, according to Crossette?
2. According to the author, what nation currently has the world's lowest fertility rate?
3. What are some exceptions to the underpopulation trend cited by Crossette?

In the 200 years since Thomas Malthus published his "Essay on the Principle of Population" and threw a scare into the human race about the limits of the earth's resources, people everywhere have been asking: Are there too many of us?

This week, leading demographers from around the world will meet here to fret over a revolutionary new fear: Will there soon be too few of us?

The world's population, now at about 5.7 billion, is still growing. By the middle of the [twenty-first] century, it is likely to stand at about 9.4 billion. And although Malthus was way off the mark in predicting an early demographic disaster, there are still enough warning signs to keep neo-Malthusians busy. Last week, for example, a World Bank body joined the hardy band of worrywarts who foresee a world unable to feed all its people as crop lands and sea stocks diminish, harvest yields level off and water supplies dry up.

The Richest Nations Have the Lowest Fertility Rates

But for demographers, the problem lately is not absolute numbers of people and their pressures on the environment and natural resources. Now the experts are worried about what happens when population growth slows in a lot of places, or even stops entirely or declines in some. Fertility rates in many places are dropping rapidly, especially in the richest countries, where, to put it simply, any two people are not producing two more people.

If this trend continues it could have far-reaching consequences, demographers say. When more and more of the world's most highly industrialized and economically productive nations do not replenish their numbers, their role as engines of global growth—both as producers and consumers of goods—is thrown into doubt.

"These developed countries have a particularly important role because they provide a great deal of the economic leadership and social leadership," said Joseph Chamie, director of the United Nations population division, which organized the conference.

"They are, basically, the producer nations, the consumer nations and the donor nations," he said. "China today is exporting to whom? Basically to the United States and Europe, and that's helping the Chinese economy. Europe alone consumes a great deal and produces a great deal. If they start shrinking there will be a readjustment, and it will be global in its impact. It will affect the entire world economy."

Unlike dips in population growth throughout history, this slide—which began in the 1960's—was not caused by a natural or economic disaster, a war or plague. There is no Black Death to blame, no World War I, no Great Depression. This decline is widespread. It is steady. And while no demographer would say that predictions are infallible—prognosticators have sure been wrong in the past, and humanity is of course adaptable—the current decline shows no signs of reversing as earlier ones have.

More Migration from the Third World to the First

Demographers believe that fundamental social changes explain the fact that people in more and more places are having fewer kids. The changes include urbanization—there's less incentive to have a big family in the city—and global migrations, in which men are typically separated from wives, and migrants are exposed to modernizing influences. And, of course, women have greater power over their own lives.

The declines are uneven, with the fertility rates of poorer nations slower to drop to the level that demographers say is needed simply to maintain a given nation's current population total—2.1 children per woman on average—a level below which much of the industrialized world has already fallen.

The third world's higher fertility rates help explain why some developing countries with surplus labor have begun to campaign for the right of workers to migrate freely in search of jobs. As labor forces shrink in richer nations, it will be hard to keep them out, as Europe has tried to do with limited success. Meanwhile, waves of migrations from Europe—the sort that largely shaped the modern world—have ceased.

In the United States, where migration from the third world is high, the new arrivals have already changed American society, with fewer Europeans and more people from other regions crossing oceans and land borders in search of better times. The United States hovers just above the replacement fertility rate, but its population is growing more rapidly than those of other industrial nations because of immigration.

Europe Will Be Profoundly Affected

Europe was the first region to slide below the 2.1-children-per-woman replacement level—that is, two new people to take the places of the mother and father, plus a little slack to account for childhood deaths. Italy has the world's lowest fertility rate, 1.2, followed by Spain and Germany at 1.3. Even Ireland, a country with a fertility rate of 3.55 in 1975, has seen its rate drop markedly, to 1.87 by 1995.

The Economic Implications of Underpopulation

There is not the slightest sign of a new baby boom in any developed country. But even if birthrates increased overnight to the three-plus figure of the U.S. baby boom of 50 years ago, it would take 25 years before those new babies would become fully educated and productive adults. For the next 25 years . . . the underpopulation of the developed countries is accomplished fact and thus has the following implications for their societies and economics:

• Actual retirement age—the age at which people stop working—will go up in all developed countries to 75 for healthy people, who are the great majority. That rise in retirement age will occur well before the year 2010.

• Economic growth can no longer come from either putting more people to work—that is, from more resource input, as much of it has come in the past—or from greater consumer demand. It can come only from a very sharp and continuing increase in the productivity of the one resource in which the developed countries still have an edge (and which they are likely to maintain for a few more decades): the productivity of knowledge work and of knowledge workers.

Peter Drucker, *The Futurist*, November 1998.

"Socially and economically, Ireland has changed substantially in recent decades," say James McCarthy and Jo Murphy-Lawless, who prepared a study for the conference here. They cite higher Irish education levels, a new, less isolationist world view fostered by membership in the European Union, economic growth and the eroding influence of the Roman Catholic Church.

In Italy, government officials foresee empty classrooms and thousands of unemployed teachers, with shortages of service industry workers and health-care personnel to care for older people. Politicians in a number of countries will have to factor in the numerical power and thus ballot-box clout of older citizens, who are often a conservative force. In the United States, older people heavily influence debates over the future of Social Security, Medicaid and the setting of other priorities in national budgets.

Some Nations Are Trying Pronatalist Policies

Several European and Asian governments are taking steps to fight the low-fertility trend. Italy has parliamentary committees looking into ways to make it easier for women to have careers and children simultaneously. France, while no longer awarding medals for motherhood, does pay child allowances and provides a range of help for families willing to grow. Sweden, South Korea and Malaysia have created incentives also, and Singapore set up a bureaucracy to figure out ways to bring singles together.

Ryuichi Kaneko of Japan's National Institute of Population and Social Security Research says Japan's economy will have to adapt to a smaller labor force. Japan faces not only a change in population structure but also its size. By the time its fertility rate levels off in 2007, Japanese society will be older on average than most European populations, and the nation's population will see a steady decline in numbers for the first time in its history.

Worldwide, the number of countries with below-replacement fertility in 1970 was 19, almost all in Europe or North America. By 1995, there were 51 countries on the below-replacement chart, with new arrivals including nations of east and southeast Asia, the Caribbean and Eastern Europe. By 2015, demographers estimate, 88 of the world's more than 180 countries and territories will have replacement levels at or below 2.1 children per woman.

Exceptions to the trend are found in Africa, especially sub-Saharan Africa, some areas of the Middle East, South Asia and

West Asia. Pakistan, for example, is likely to be the world's third most populous country by 2050 unless it can trim its high growth rate. By then neighboring India, with its laissez-faire family planning policy, will likely outstrip China in population to rank first, while the United States will be fourth. But some demographers think it is only a matter of time before the forces of change are felt even in the poorest countries.

"As in other spheres of global international life, there seem to be powerful globalizing forces at work pushing towards fertility reduction," says Jean-Claude Chesnais of the National Institute of Demographic Studies in Paris. He thinks historical patterns may offer little as a guide. "The future is not a simple replication of the past," he wrote in a paper for the conference. "Present societies are much more complex than ancient ones."

Mr. Chamie thinks something more fundamental may be in the air. In preoccupations with subjects as diverse as threats to the global environment or the reproductive rights of women, he said, "we have talked fertility down."

"Concerns about cancer, heart disease, and other illnesses . . . may be alleviated, only to be replaced by the threat of a population explosion in which the extraordinarily long-lived elderly become an overwhelming social problem."

Increases in Life Expectancy Could Cause a Population Explosion

William B. Schwartz

William B. Schwartz is a professor of medicine at the University of Southern California, a fellow at the Pacific Center for Health Policy and Ethics, and the author of *Life Without Disease: The Pursuit of Medical Utopia*. In the following viewpoint, Schwartz predicts that advances in medical research could increase average human life expectancy to well over 120 years. Because such a development would result in fewer deaths, but no fewer births, he warns that it could result in a population explosion.

As you read, consider the following questions:
1. What does the author say is the fastest growing segment of the U.S. population?
2. According to Schwartz, how might scientists be able to prevent programmed cell death?
3. What does the author believe is the most likely near-term response to overpopulation?

Excerpted from "The Conquest of Disease: It's Almost Within Sight," by William B. Schwartz, originally published in *The Futurist*, January 1999. Reprinted with permission from the World Future Society, 7910 Woodmont Ave., Suite 450, Bethesda, MD 20814. Telephone: (301) 951-0394; Fax: (301) 951-0394; www.wfs.org/wfs.

Exactly where we will stand in the long war against disease by the year 2050 is impossible to say. But if developments in research maintain their current pace, it seems likely that a combination of improved attention to dietary and environmental factors, along with advances in gene therapy and protein-targeted drugs, will have virtually eliminated most major classes of disease.

From an economic standpoint, the best news may be that these accomplishments could be accompanied by a drop in health-care costs. Costs may even fall as diseases are brought under control using pinpointed, short-term therapies now being developed. By 2050 there will be fewer hospitals, and surgical procedures will be largely restricted to the treatment of accidents and other forms of trauma. Spending on nonacute care, both in nursing facilities and in homes, will also fall sharply as more elderly people lead healthy lives until close to death.

One result of medicine's success in controlling disease will be a dramatic increase in life expectancy. The extent of that increase is a highly speculative matter, but it is worth noting that medical science has already helped to make the very old (currently defined as those over 85 years of age) the fastest-growing segment of the population. Between 1960 and 1995, the U.S. population as a whole increased by about 45%, while the segment over 85 years of age grew by almost 300%. There has been a similar explosion in the population of centenarians, with the result that survival to the age of 100 is no longer the newsworthy feat that it was only a few decades ago. U.S. Census Bureau projections already forecast dramatic increases in the number of centenarians in the next 50 years: 4 million in 2050, compared with 37,000 in 1990.

Although Census Bureau calculations project an increase in average life-span of only eight years by the year 2050, some experts believe that the human life-span should not begin to encounter any theoretical natural limits before 120 years. With continuing advances in molecular medicine and a growing understanding of the aging process, that limit could rise to 130 years or more.

Aging is typically accompanied by increased vulnerability to illness, but it also exhibits physical manifestations that are not connected to any particular disease process. Characteristic signs include diminished appetite, general muscle weakness and unsteadiness of gait, thinning of the skin, and decreases in lung and kidney function. These changes contribute to the overall frailty of old age and are indicators of a slow process of withering away, even in the absence of an identifiable disease. This elusive process will be the object of intense scrutiny in the decades ahead.

Researchers have already gained much insight from the study of Werner's syndrome, a rare genetic disorder in which the normal aging clock is dramatically and disastrously accelerated. The disease results in the uncanny phenomenon of patients in their teens and 20s with gray hair, cataracts, atrophied muscles, and loss of bone mass that would be normal only for the very old. Skin biopsies reveal tissue structure very similar to those of the aged, and cells demonstrate a sharply diminished ability to replicate.

The premature aging and early death of Werner's patients, once an enigma, now appears to be the result of a defective gene that induces production of an abnormal helicase protein. This protein interferes with the body's normal process of DNA repair, the failure of which seems to be a key feature of premature aging. Defective helicase also appears to cause widespread damage that results in cancer, early heart disease, and rare skin diseases. Identification of the roles of helicase and DNA repair in the bizarrely accelerated aging process of Werner's syndrome has obvious implications for our understanding of normal aging.

Meanwhile, researchers studying roundworms have demonstrated that four genes, when mutated, cause the roundworm to live almost five times longer than its natural life expectancy—nearly two months rather than the normal nine days. Worms with this "long life" mutation have a lower metabolic rate, eat and move more languidly, and generally exhibit a more placid pace of life. (Is there a lesson for humans here?)

Interpretations of these findings vary. Some researchers suggest that the "rate of living" is a key determinant of degeneration and death. A slower life, it is thought, may reduce the rate at which the body produces toxic oxidative byproducts of metabolism (free radicals) that damage DNA. Other researchers believe that a slower life may allow damaged DNA to be more readily repaired. Although these explanations are speculative, it seems clear that a genetic alteration can in fact extend life.

Research for a Longer Life

The first attempt to slow down the wear and tear of aging has focused on helping the body eliminate the highly reactive free radical molecules that inflict damage on DNA, cell proteins, and other critical biological substances. The body has its own defenses against free radicals, including naturally occurring antioxidants. To boost these defenses, researchers have suggested that a variety of supplementary antioxidants—including vitamins C and E, beta-carotene, and selenium—be used as therapies. Antioxidant administration in animals modestly extends life, but there is no evidence that current antioxidant supplements have a similar effect in humans. Still, antioxidant therapy is a landmark in the acceptance of aging as a treatable condition.

An important biological phenomenon, programmed cell death, opens another avenue of exploration. Normal cells grown in a test tube can divide no more than about 50 times before a "cell death" program is activated. The program is apparently triggered by the loss of telomere from the caps at the ends of each chromosome. These caps protect the genes in the chromosome from injury and allow cell division to proceed normally. As cells divide, the telomere cap shortens at each replication, and when the cap shortens sufficiently, a signal blocks further multiplication of the cell, and it dies. Can this loss of telomeres be prevented, and the cells thereby kept from aging and dying?

The most promising approach to preserving telomeres focuses on the naturally occurring enzyme telomerase, which has the capacity to synthesize new caps on chromosomes. Techniques for stimulating telomerase activity may therefore maintain the integrity of telomere caps, prolong the life of cells, and extend the life of the organism—so long as uncontrolled, cancerous cell growth can be avoided.

Because aging involves many factors, it is unlikely that

An Older World

With the continuation of fertility decline and increase in life expectancy, the population of the world will age much faster in the next half-century than previously. The median age increased from 23.5 years in 1950 to 26.4 years in 1999. By 2050, the median age is projected to reach 37.8 years.

The proportion of children, less than 15 years old, declined from 34 per cent in 1950 to 30 per cent in 1999 while the proportion of older persons, aged 60 or over, increased from 8 to 10 per cent over the same period. By 2050, it is expected, according to the medium variant projection, that the proportion of children will have declined by one-third of its 1999 level, to 20 per cent, and that the proportion of older persons will have more than doubled, to 22 per cent, exceeding the proportion of children for the first time in human history. . . .

The number of working age persons per older person is declining rapidly. The potential support ratio (the number of persons aged 15–64 years per older person aged 65 years or older) indicates the dependency burden on potential workers. The impact of demographic ageing is visible in the potential support ratio, which is falling in both more and less developed regions. Between 1999 and 2050, the potential support ratio will decline from 5 working age persons per older person to 2 working age persons per older person in more developed regions, and in less developed regions from 12 to 4 working age persons per older person.

United Nations, *The World at Six Billion*, 1999.

---

telomerase activation alone will be the "magic cure" for senescence. But taken together with the discoveries concerning the effects of free radicals and of the helicase protein's role in Werner's disease, the findings suggest that we are entering a new era in the understanding of aging. Whether this work will lead to major changes in our clinical understanding and control of aging and its diseases is still not clear. But conceivably by 2050, aging may in fact prove to be simply another disease to be treated.

The Social Consequences of an Extended Life-Span

Every change in human society, no matter how seemingly beneficial, brings with it the potential for new problems, and the continuing conquest of human disease is no exception.

Concerns about cancer, heart disease, and other illnesses—and the costs of associated health care—may be alleviated, only to be replaced by the threat of a population explosion in which the extraordinarily long-lived elderly become an overwhelming social problem.

Overpopulation as a threat to mankind is not a new issue. As early as 1800, Thomas Malthus argued that, because of the natural exponential growth of populations, a stable population could be maintained only through wars, famine, and plague—or, less plausibly, through voluntary "moral restraint." But overpopulation surfaced as a major policy concern around 1960 and attracted wide attention with the publication of an influential report by the Club of Rome dealing with the limits to population growth and of Paul Ehrlich's widely read book, *The Population Bomb*.

High birthrates were initially held to be the root of the population crisis. But as long ago as the 1950s—just about the time that the DNA double helix was discovered—science-fiction writers began to envision the time when overpopulation would result from the life-extending miracles of modern medicine. In his 1953 short story, "Tomorrow and Tomorrow and Tomorrow," Kurt Vonnegut Jr. presents a humorous but believable vision of a society paralyzed by the burden of an older generation that has worn out its welcome, as typified by this exchange:

"Sometimes I get so mad, I feel like just up and diluting his anti-gerasone," said Em.

"That'd be against Nature, Em," said Lou, "it'd be murder. Besides, if he caught us tinkering with his anti-gerasone, not only would he disinherit us, he'd bust my neck. Just because he's one hundred and seventy-two doesn't mean Gramps isn't strong as a bull."

"Against Nature," said Em. "Who knows what Nature's like anymore? Ohhhh—I don't guess I could ever bring myself to dilute his anti-gerasone or anything like that, but, gosh, Lou, a body can't help thinking Gramps is never going to leave if somebody doesn't help him along a little. Golly—we're so crowded a person can hardly turn around, and Verna's dying for a baby, and Melissa's gone thirty years without one." She stamped her feet. "I get so sick of seeing his wrinkled old face, watching him take the only private room and the best chair and the best food, and getting to pick out what to watch on TV, and running everybody's life by changing his will all the time."

Images of Extended Life

The widely discussed film *Soylent Green*, made in 1973 and based on a 1966 short story by Harry Harrison, depicts a macabre program of mass extermination as a way to deal with the overpopulation caused by medical progress. Many other science-fiction works of the 1960s and 1970s depict organized euthanasia as a solution to the problem: The victims are chosen by a variety of creative methods, ranging from random lottery to selective culling of the old, infirm, or politically suspect. In some of the most chilling scenarios, medical professionals assist in the killing.

In one story, for instance, 10% of the supplies of a vaccine are replaced with a placebo in order to permit a randomly selected portion of the population to be eliminated through infectious disease. Only slightly less grotesque are the short stories that imagine enforced restrictions on reproduction as a way out of the overpopulation dilemma. Jose Farmer's 1985 novel, *Dayworld*, offers yet another approach to the problem: He envisions a world in which every person is conscious for only one day per week, spending the other six days stacked in a storage facility (a tactic that contemporary office workers might argue has already been enacted).

These imaginative speculations offer few practical lessons, but they show that thoughtful people have begun to consider medical advancement as a two-edged sword—not only because of the economic consequences, but also because it threatens to distort the natural cycle of birth, aging, and death. Although restrictions on reproductive freedom or a mandated approach to euthanasia may seem unthinkable today, in another 50 years the population problem may be so severe that all conceivable solutions will be considered.

Perhaps the most likely near-term response to overpopulation is that government policy makers will direct medical research funding toward work that increases the quality of life, rather than its length. Research funding for some of the genetic interventions discussed earlier could be curtailed, in favor of attention to such problems as loss of hearing and eyesight, degenerative skin diseases, and other infirmities of old age. Even this relatively benign strategy for slowing the rise in life expectancy would be likely to encounter strong opposition, and of course any deliberate stifling of scientific progress is a cause for concern. We can only hope that, as the contours of the dilemma become clearer in the decades ahead, creative minds will forge solutions that can avoid the world of Vonnegut's imagining.

It could be that life-extending medical progress will eventually plateau for purely scientific reasons, but the medical successes of recent decades provide ample reason for us to plan for the possibility of a world in which disease and death are pushed ever farther into the second century of life.

Periodical Bibliography

The following articles have been selected to supplement the diverse views presented in this chapter. Addresses are provided for periodicals not indexed in the *Readers' Guide to Periodical Literature*, the *Alternative Press Index*, the *Social Sciences Index*, or the *Index to Legal Periodicals and Books*.

Lester Brown	"Reassessing the Earth's Population," *Society*, May/June 1995.
Joel E. Cohen	"Ten Myths of Population," *Discover*, April 1996.
Shanti R. Conly	"Sub-Saharan Africa: At the Turning Point," *Humanist*, July/August 1998.
Barbara Crossette	"Rethinking Population at a Global Milestone," *New York Times*, September 19, 1999.
Werner Fornos	"No Vacancy," *Humanist*, July/August 1998.
William G. Hollingsworth	"Population Explosion: Still Expanding," *USA Today*, July 1998.
Steven E. Landsburg	"The More, the Merrier," *Forbes*, May 22, 1995.
Joseph A. McFalls Jr.	"Population: A Lively Introduction," *Population Bulletin*, September 1998.
Bill McKibben	"The Future of Population: A Special Moment in History," *Atlantic Monthly*, May 1998.
Anne S. Moffat	"Ecologists Look at the Big Picture: Method for Estimating Largest Population That Can Live on Earth," *Science*, September 13, 1996.
John S. Morton, Jane S. Shaw, and Richard L. Stroup	"Overpopulation: Where Malthus Went Wrong," *Social Education*, October 1997.
Thomas T. Poleman	"Past Growth and Future Control," *Population and Environment*, Spring 1995.
Max Singer	"The Population Surprise," *Atlantic Monthly*, August 1999.

CHAPTER 3

How Serious a Problem Is Overpopulation?

Chapter Preface

One problem that has traditionally been associated with population is disease. Epidemiologists, who study the spread of disease, have long known that disease is linked to areas with high population density. This is not only because disease spreads faster in areas with lots of people, but also because crowded urban areas are more prone to having poor sanitary conditions that facilitate the spread of disease.

In contrast to the epidemiological study of how population density affects disease, demographers have traditionally studied how disease affects population. Simply put, disease reduces population. History's most infamous example of this is the Black Death, which killed between one-fourth and one-third of Europe's population in the years 1347–1350. But even in early-twentieth-century America, diseases such as tuberculosis, cholera, smallpox, and polio remained major sources of mortality.

Since World War II, medical advances such as the development of vaccines and the discovery of antibiotics have resulted in major decreases in the world's overall mortality rate. With the infectious diseases listed above seemingly vanquished, many scientists assumed that disease would have a negligible effect on global population in the twenty-first century.

However, recent work by researcher Laurie Garrett suggests that infectious disease could once again have a major negative impact on the world's population. In her view, many factors, including the overuse of penicillin (and the drug-resistant microbes that have resulted from this overuse), increased densities of the human population caused by worldwide urbanization, and the incredible increase in worldwide travel, may help contribute to potentially lethal epidemics.

Disease is just one of the problems associated with overpopulation. Food shortages, widespread poverty, and many environmental problems have also been blamed on the human species' capacity for rapid growth. The authors in the following chapter debate whether these problems are caused by overpopulation or by other factors.

> "[Overpopulation], combined with rising
> individual consumption, is pushing our . . .
> planet beyond its natural limits."

Increased Population Is Causing a Global Ecological Disaster

Lester R. Brown, Gary Gardner, and Brian Halweil

Lester R. Brown is founder, president, and senior researcher at the Worldwatch Institute in Washington, D.C., an organization that studies global environmental problems. Gary Gardner is also a senior researcher at the institute, and Brian Halweil is a staff researcher. In the following viewpoint, they list eleven possible negative consequences that overpopulation could have on the environment, and maintain that these consequences warrant an immediate worldwide effort to stabilize human population.

As you read, consider the following questions:
1. To what do the authors attribute the slow growth in the world's grain harvest?
2. According to the authors, what percentage of global forests have been lost in the twentieth century?
3. By how much has world oil declined since 1979, according to Brown, Gardner, and Halweil?

Excerpted from "Increased Population Is Causing a Global Ecological Disaster," by Lester R. Brown, Gary Gardner, and Brian Halweil, originally published in *The Futurist*, February 1999. Reprinted with permission from the World Future Society, 7910 Woodmont Ave., Suite 450, Bethesda, MD 20814. Telephone: (301) 951-0394; Fax: (301) 951-0394; www.wfs.org/wfs.

The world's population has doubled during the last half century, climbing from 2.5 billion in 1950 to 5.9 billion in 1998. This unprecedented surge in population, combined with rising individual consumption, is pushing our claims on the planet beyond its natural limits.

The United Nations projects that human population in 2050 will range between 7.7 billion and 11.2 billion people. We use the United Nations' middle-level projection of 9.4 billion (from *World Population Prospects: The 1996 Revision*) to give an idea of the strain this "most likely" outcome would place on ecosystems and governments in the future and of the urgent need to break from the business-as-usual scenario. . . .

Farming and Fresh Water

1. Grain production. From 1950 to 1984, growth in the world grain harvest easily exceeded that of population. But since then, the growth in the grain harvest has fallen behind that of population, so per-person output has dropped by 7% (0.5% a year), according to the U.S. Department of Agriculture.

The slower growth in the world grain harvest since 1984 is due to the lack of new land and to slower growth in irrigation and fertilizer use because of the diminishing returns of these inputs.

Now that the frontiers of agricultural settlement have disappeared, future growth in grain production must come almost entirely from raising land productivity. Unfortunately, this is becoming more difficult. The challenge for the world's farmers is to reverse this decline at a time when cropland area per person is shrinking, the amount of irrigation water per person is dropping, and the crop yield response to additional fertilizer use is falling.

2. Cropland. Since mid-century, grain area—which serves as a proxy for cropland in general—has increased by some 19%, but global population has grown by 132%. Population growth can degrade farmland, reducing its productivity or even eliminating it from production. As grain area per person falls, more and more nations risk losing the capacity to feed themselves.

The trend is illustrated starkly in the world's four fastest-growing large countries. Having already seen per capita grain area shrink by 40%–50% between 1960 and 1998, Pakistan, Nigeria, Ethiopia, and Iran can expect a further 60%–70% loss by 2050—a conservative projection that assumes no further losses of agricultural land. The result will be four countries with a combined population of more than 1 billion whose grain area per person will be only 300–600 square meters—less than a quarter of the area in 1950.

3. *Fresh water.* Spreading water scarcity may be the most underrated resource issue in the world today. Wherever population is growing, the supply of fresh water per person is declining.

Evidence of water stress can be seen as rivers are drained dry and water tables fall. Rivers such as the Nile, the Yellow, and the Colorado have little water left when they reach the sea. Water tables are now falling on every continent, including in major food-producing regions. Aquifers are being depleted in the U.S. southern Great Plains, the North China Plain, and most of India.

The International Water Management Institute projects that a billion people will be living in countries facing absolute water scarcity by 2025. These countries will have to reduce water use in agriculture in order to satisfy residential and industrial water needs. In both China and India, the two countries that together dominate world irrigated agriculture, substantial cutbacks in irrigation water supplies lie ahead.

Fish and Livestock

4. *Oceanic fish catch.* A fivefold growth in the human appetite for seafood since 1950 has pushed the catch of most oceanic fisheries to their sustainable limits or beyond. Marine biologists believe that the oceans cannot sustain an annual catch of much more than 93 million tons, the current take.

As we near the end of the twentieth century, overfishing has become the rule, not the exception. Of the 15 major oceanic fisheries, 11 are in decline. The catch of Atlantic cod—long a dietary mainstay for western Europeans—has fallen by 70% since peaking in 1968. Since 1970, bluefin tuna stocks in the West Atlantic have dropped by 80%.

With the oceans now pushed to their limits, future growth in the demand for seafood can be satisfied only by fish farming. But as the world turns to aquaculture to satisfy its needs, fish begin to compete with livestock and poultry for feedstuffs such as grain, soybean meal, and fish meal.

The next half century is likely to be marked by the disappearance of some species from markets, a decline in the quality of seafood caught, higher prices, and more conflicts among countries over access to fisheries. Each year, the future oceanic catch per person will decline by roughly the amount of population growth, dropping to 9.9 kilograms (22 pounds) per person in 2050, compared with the 1988 peak of 17.2 kilograms (37.8 pounds).

5. *Meat production.* When incomes begin to rise in traditional low-income societies, one of the first things people do is diversify their diets, consuming more livestock products.

World meat production since 1950 has increased almost twice as fast as population. Growth in meat production was originally concentrated in western industrial countries and Japan, but over the last two decades it has increased rapidly in East Asia, the Middle East, and Latin America. Beef, pork, and poultry account for the bulk of world consumption.

Of the world grain harvest of 1.87 billion tons in 1998, an estimated 37% will be used to feed livestock and poultry, producing milk and eggs as well as meat, according to the U.S. Department of Agriculture. Grain fed to livestock and poultry is now the principal food reserve in the event of a world food emergency.

Total meat consumption will rise from 211 million tons in 1997 to 513 million tons in 2050, increasing pressures on the supply of grain.

Impacts on the Environment

6. *Natural recreation areas.* From Buenos Aires to Bangkok, dramatic population growth in the world's major cities—and the sprawl and pollution they bring—threaten natural recreation areas that lie beyond city limits. On every continent, human encroachment has reduced both the size and the quality of natural recreation areas.

In nations where rapid population growth has outstripped the carrying capacity of local resources, protected areas become especially vulnerable. Although in industrial nations these areas are synonymous with camping, hiking, and picnics in the country, in Asia, Africa, and Latin America most national parks, forests, and preserves are inhabited or used for natural resources by local populations.

Migration-driven population growth also endangers natural recreation areas in many industrial nations. Everglades National Park, for example, faces collapse as millions of newcomers move into southern Florida.

Longer waiting lists and higher user fees for fewer secluded spots are likely to be the tip of the iceberg, as population growth threatens to eliminate the diversity of habitats and cultures, in addition to the peace and quiet, that protected areas currently offer.

7. *Forests.* Global losses of forest area have marched in step with population growth for much of human history, but an estimated 75% of the loss in global forests has occurred in the twentieth century.

In Latin America, ranching is the single largest cause of deforestation. In addition, overgrazing and overcollection of firewood—which are often a function of growing population—are degrading 14% of the world's remaining large areas of virgin forest.

Deforestation created by the demand for forest products tracks closely with rising per capita consumption in recent decades. Global use of paper and paperboard per person has doubled (or nearly tripled) since 1961.

The loss of forest areas leads to a decline of forest services. These include habitat for wildlife; carbon storage, which is a key to regulating climate; and erosion control, provision of water across rainy and dry seasons, and regulation of rainfall.

8. *Biodiversity.* We live amid the greatest extinction of plant and animal life since the dinosaurs disappeared 65 million years ago, at the end of the Cretaceous period, with species losses at 100 to 1,000 times the natural rate. The principal cause of species extinction is habitat loss, which tends to accelerate with an increase in a country's population density.

A particularly productive but vulnerable habitat is found in coastal areas, home to 60% of the world's population.

Coastal wetlands nurture two-thirds of all commercially caught fish, for example. And coral reefs have the second-highest concentration of biodiversity in the world, after tropical rain forests. But human encroachment and pollution are degrading these areas: Roughly half of the world's salt marshes and mangrove swamps have been eliminated or radically altered, and two-thirds of the world's coral reefs have been degraded, 10% of them "beyond recognition." As coastal migration continues—coastal dwellers could account for 75% of world population within 30 years—the pressures on these productive habitats will likely increase.

Population and the Environment

Human action has transformed between one-third and one-half of the entire land surface of the earth. We have lost more than one-quarter of the planet's birds, and two-thirds of the major marine fisheries are fully exploited, over-exploited or depleted.

Every 20 minutes, the world adds another 3,500 human lives but loses one or more entire species of animal or plant life—at least 27,000 species per year. This is a rate and scale of extinction that has not occurred in 65 million years. . . .

Clearly, the greatest environmental threat comes from both the wealthiest billion people, who consume the most and generate the most waste, and from the poorest billion, who may damage their meager resource base in the daily struggle to avoid starvation. In addition, the billions in between are doing their best to increase their standard of living, in part through increased consumption.

Zero Population Growth, *Population and the Environment*, 1999.

---

9. Climate change. Over the last half century, carbon emissions from fossil-fuel burning expanded at nearly twice the rate of population, boosting atmospheric concentrations of carbon dioxide, the principal greenhouse gas, by 30% over preindustrial levels.

Fossil-fuel use accounts for roughly three-quarters of world carbon emissions. As a result, regional growth in carbon emissions tends to occur where economic activity and related energy use is projected to grow most rapidly. Emissions in China are projected to grow over three times faster than population in the next 50 years due to a booming economy that is heavily reliant on coal and other carbon-rich energy sources.

Emissions from developing countries will nearly quadruple over the next half century, while those from industrial nations will increase by 30%, according to the Intergovernmental Panel on Climate Change and the U.S. Department of Energy. Although annual emissions from industrial countries are currently twice as high as from developing ones, the latter are on target to eclipse the industrial world by 2020.

Less Fuel and More Waste

10. Energy. The global demand for energy grew twice as fast as population over the last 50 years. By 2050, developing countries will be consuming much more energy as their populations increase and become more affluent.

When per capita energy consumption is high, even a low rate of population growth can have significant effects on total energy demand. In the United States, for example, the 75 million people projected to be added to the population by 2050 will boost energy demand to roughly the present energy consumption of Africa and Latin America.

World oil production per person reached a high in 1979 and has since declined by 23%. Estimates of when global oil production will peak range from 2011 to 2025, signaling future price shocks as long as oil remains the world's dominant fuel.

In the next 50 years, the greatest growth in energy demands will come where economic activity is projected to be highest: in Asia, where consumption is expected to grow 361%, though population will grow by just 50%. Energy consumption is also expected to increase in Latin America (by 340%) and Africa (by 326%). In all three regions, local pressures on energy sources, ranging from forests to fossil-fuel reserves to waterways, will be significant.

11. Waste. Local and global environmental effects of waste disposal will likely worsen as 3.4 billion people are added to the world's population over the next half century. Prospects for providing access to sanitation are dismal in the near to medium term.

A growing population increases society's disposal headaches—the garbage, sewage, and industrial waste that must be gotten rid of. Even where population is largely stable—the case in many industrialized countries—the flow of waste products into landfills and waterways generally continues to increase. Where high rates of economic and population growth coincide in coming decades, as they will in many developing countries, mountains of waste will likely pose difficult disposal challenges for municipal and national authorities. . . .

World Population Must Be Stabilized

As we look to the future, the challenge for world leaders is to help countries maximize the prospects for achieving sustainability by keeping both birth and death rates low. In a world where both grain output and fish catch per person are falling, a strong case can be made on humanitarian grounds to stabilize world population.

"Generations of schoolchildren have been taught the wrong lessons about population, and even the State Department has been duped."

Increased Population Is Not Causing a Global Ecological Disaster

Timothy W. Maier

In the following viewpoint, Timothy W. Maier, a writer for *Insight on the News*, contends that warnings of impending disasters caused by overpopulation are merely the unfounded threats of overzealous "doomsayers." In the author's view, past predictions that overpopulation would lead to famine, global warming, and worse living conditions have been grossly inaccurate; food production, environmental problems, and living conditions have all improved in the last century. Nevertheless, says Maier, pessimists continue to frighten the public with spurious claims that a global disaster is imminent.

As you read, consider the following questions:
1. In Maier's view, what are some of the motives of those who propagate doomsday predictions?
2. What does Ben Wattenberg feel is the major problem with Paul Ehrlich's predictions about overpopulation, as paraphrased by the author?
3. What award does Alan Caruba of the National Anxiety Center present each year?

The world will end this year. True, the tabloids predicted that last year, but maybe they were right and we all are in hell. Maybe. And maybe the doomsayers are crazy.

Doomsaying certainly is popular enough. Public-opinion surveys show Americans believe the environment is dirtier, natural resources are scarcer and the population is exploding. No wonder taxpayers seem willing to reach deeply into their pockets to fund every new "Save the World" crusade that comes along.

Most of the Bad News Is Wrong

Of course the doomsayers were wrong as recently as October 1997, when the Cassini space probe safely blasted off for Saturn with its 72 pounds of plutonium. In case you missed it, the launch didn't kill everyone on the planet, as some environmentalists predicted. They were as wrong as when they projected during the seventies that the population would explode and produce global famine. That same decade they warned that soon there would not be a single tree left standing in the United States and Europe, a prediction belied by increases in forested area.

Even pesticides turned out not to be the world-ending danger portrayed in Rachel Carson's 1962 book *Silent Spring*. And today, operating on similar doomsday propaganda, the world's leaders have just met in Kyoto, Japan, to save the world from global warming—yet another scare about which there is no scientific consensus, just as there was no consensus on the global-cooling scare of several years ago.

The good news is that most of the bad news is wrong, with predictions of world-ending disaster proving to be premature—by a billion or so years. But for some, assured that the sky was falling, panic set in about DDT, alar, cellular phones, irradiated foods, nuclear power, high-voltage lines, radon, asbestos, deforestation and much more. Why are we so vulnerable to what might be called the superstition of the movement experts?

Blame the propagation of unfounded fears on disinformation campaigns bought and paid for by special-interest groups, accepted by politicians anxious to expand the power and authority of government, and perpetuated by editors looking for a doomsday headline. Or perhaps the *New England Journal of Medicine* is correct. It suggests that much of this unsubstantiated fear can be traced to "chemophobia," which is the unreasonable fear of chemicals.

Ronald Bailey, author of *Eco-Scam*, says the media deserve part of the blame because "if there is no problem, there is no news. Why do people focus on bad news? Because bad news is the stuff that can kill you right now and good news you can think about tomorrow." But nationally syndicated columnist Alston Chase says too much blame is placed on the media: "Rather than blame journalists, editors and television producers for persistent refusal to confront reality, perhaps we should consider that these folk would not be hyping doomsday if it didn't sell."

Dire Forecasts About Overpopulation Are Not True

Many experts trace the birth of doomsdayism among political liberals to Stanford economics professor Paul Ehrlich's world view touted in his best-selling 1968 book, *The Population Bomb*. The premise expanded on theories proposed in 1798 by the Rev. Thomas Malthus who, without allowing for the industrial revolution and its effects on agriculture, warned that according to his calculations the human race was about to reproduce faster than the food supply. In his 1990 follow-up book, *The Population Explosion*, Ehrlich was still at it, declaring: "Any more stuff in the world should not go to the likes of us. The world can't afford more Americans. Rich nations will now have to pay for their greed."

His solutions? Make government bigger, expand regulation, increase foreign aid, encourage abortion, restrict family choice, double the price of gasoline, etc. If these measures were not taken, Ehrlich predicted famines, wars, an end to growth in poor countries and ever greater human misery. As he said so many times as a frequent guest of Johnny Carson: "The cancer of population growth must be cut out or we will breed ourselves into oblivion."

Twenty years after Ehrlich's dire forecasts, there has been no universal famine, poor countries such as India are flourishing and peace among nations is greater than ever. In fact, without federal policing of the bedroom, recent evidence suggests that fertility rates are dropping. So what does the population guru have to say now?

Here's Ehrlich: "Unless we have a big increase in the death rate, all of the projections, even the most optimistic, show us adding another two-and-a-half billion people." "It is slowing, but we are already in a situation of near disaster. And the concern within the entire scientific community is, of course, that unless we do a lot of things right, and start pretty quick, we're going to be in deep trouble."

Not true, says Ben J. Wattenberg, a senior fellow at the American Enterprise Institute, moderator of the PBS program *Think Tank* and author of *The Birth Dearth*. He says generations of schoolchildren have been taught the wrong lessons about population, and even the State Department has been duped. And Ehrlich? "He has never been right," Wattenberg says. What is most frightening about Ehrlich is the support he receives.

Plenty of Room

Planet Earth is loaded with room. We could put the world's entire population into the United States. Doing so would make our population density 1,531 people per square mile. That's a far lower population density than what now exists in New York (11,440), Los Angeles (9,126) and Houston (7,512). The entire U.S. population could move to Texas and each family of four would enjoy 2.9 acres of land. If the entire world's population moved to Texas, California, Colorado and Alaska, each family of four would enjoy nine-tenths of an acre of land.

Walter Williams, *Conservative Chronicle*, March 3, 1999.

Wattenberg observes that Ehrlich's 1990 book was promoted by Al Gore, who wrote for the book-jacket blurb: "The time for action is due, and past due. The Ehrlichs have written the prescription. . . ." That may prove to be a poor choice of words for the presidentially ambitious Gore, considering one of the prescriptions Ehrlich advocates is dumping chemicals in the water supply to control population, Wattenberg says.

"Look, the country with the most rapid population growth and the most economic growth is the United States—and it became an economic superpower. Generally if a place is growing it is getting wealthier," Wattenberg says. The major problem with Ehrlich's theory is that he doesn't take into account that fertility rates are declining dramatically, Wattenberg adds.

From 1950 to 1955, the average number of children born per woman per lifetime was five. By 1975 to 1980, fertility had fallen to four children per woman and, by the 1990s, the rate fell to about three and now sits at 2.8, and sinking. Wattenberg attributes the decline to more education for women, legal abortion, higher incomes, greater acceptance of homosexuality, improved contraception and later marriages.

Groundless Fears

What about the prediction of food-supply shrinkage? "Listen, I don't think there was a food-shortage problem even under the old projection," Wattenberg says. "For the new projections it is a piece of cake. There won't be a food shortage. The famine cases we had were political famines."

Decreasing birth rates reduce the threat of global warming, he adds, because scientists projected a population of 11.5 billion when determining the threat of global warming. Wattenberg calculates that the population actually will decline by the middle of the [twenty-first] century.

The threat may be balderdash but that is not comforting to Ehrlich and environmentalists such as recent Zero Population Growth award winners Ted Turner and Jane Fonda, who advocate limiting parents to just one child and never miss an opportunity to ring the tocsin against global warming. But no doubt Ted and Jane can be forgiven for being taken in by the scientism of some of the credentialed naysayers. Their predictions, after all, are horrific.

For instance, Ehrlich says of the alleged population bomb, "There's maybe a 10 percent chance we'll get away with it and maybe a 10 percent chance that it will essentially destroy civilization. And the issue for the public is, what kind of insurance do you want to take out against maybe a 10 percent chance of your grandchildren not having a prayer?"

Compare the tone of that "10 percent chance" with the declaration of Warren Leon of the Washington-based

Union of Concerned Scientists, a left-wing interest group, who says, "The chances of global warming happening are quite high. And because of this serious threat, and the high chances of it happening, we should take action to do something about it."

Alan Caruba, founder of the Maplewood, New Jersey–based National Anxiety Center, criticizes such groups for distorting scientific fact and creating mass hysteria. Caruba publishes a guide to bogus environmental claims with this advice: "The Earth is Fine. Save Yourself." Each year he presents "Chicken Little Awards" to honor individuals and groups who have scared the living daylights out of millions of Americans, including the Sierra Club, the Environmental Protection Agency, Worldwatch Institute and People for the Ethical Treatment of Animals.

"Many of the most commonly accepted threats to Earth and humanity have very little basis in scientific fact," says Caruba. "The result is that buzzwords like acid rain, global warming and ozone loss have a credibility that lacks scientific accuracy. The cost of legislation based on inaccurate or nonexistent scientific merit is incalculable."

Doomsayers Persist with Their Predictions

That doesn't matter to polemical doomsayers who are convinced the world is headed for a major crash. And for years they have been able to grab the ear of the highest office in the land. Consider this authoritative assessment prepared by some of the world's most celebrated (and politicized) scientists two decades ago. Their *1980 Global 2000 Report* to President Carter states:

"If present trends continue, the world in 2000 will be more crowded, more polluted, less stable ecologically and more vulnerable to disruption than the world we live in now. Serious stresses involving population, resources and environment are clearly visible ahead. Despite greater material output, the world's people will be poorer in many ways than they are today."

Could we find someone who would wager that this doomsday prediction is right on the money? There would be no takers, says [the late] University of Maryland professor Julian L.

Simon, who studies population and economic issues and is an adjunct scholar at the Cato Institute. Why not? Because those predictions are bunk, says Simon, who recently finished editing the book, *The State of Humanity*, in which scholars challenge many of the doomsayers' scare scenarios. Simon says those who claim the world was far better off a century ago are mistaken, and he is so sure of it he is willing to bet $100,000 that the doomsayers' predictions are off target.

"You pick any place in the world and any date in the future and I'll bet you the world shows improvement rather than deterioration," says Simon. "The doomsayers won't put their money on the table. They find every excuse not to bet me." Nearly a decade ago, Ehrlich did take him up on a $1,000 wager involving the prices of world raw materials. Simon won.

Ehrlich still is fuming. He calls Simon "the professor of mail-order marketing," and adds, "You can always search the world, as for instance the Western Fools Association has, and find someone willing to say 'We're going to stave off the next ice age,' or as Simon once said, 'The population can grow for 7 billion more years.' That's more time than the Earth has been in existence. You can always find somebody to say something like that."

Lester R. Brown, director of the Washington-based Worldwatch Institute, is another who professes not to take Simon's bet seriously. Brown consistently predicts impending ecological doom and has forecast multiple doomsday scenarios based on social and political problems for which he offers legislative solutions. He also has predicted that government policies of which he disapproves will lead to widespread hunger and insists the Earth is deteriorating on almost every front. Brown's doomsday scenarios are quickly passed on by gullible media.

Finally, however, this sort of thing is starting to become an embarrassment to reputable scientists, who more and more have found their voice. Elizabeth M. Whelan, president of the American Council on Science and Health, or ACSH, has published a *Facts Versus Fiction* report which identifies the "20 Greatest Unfounded Health Scares of Recent Times.". . .

Whelan says scientists and doctors should continue to speak out against the polemicists. As for the public, she offers this advice in her *Facts Versus Fear* report: "The next time such an alarm flashes across your TV screen, you might just want to mutter, 'Been there; done that'—and switch the channel."

One longs for Cassandra's curse—that whatever she predicted was doomed not to be believed.

> *"In many developing countries rapid population growth makes it difficult for agricultural production to keep pace with the rising demand for food."*

Overpopulation Contributes to World Hunger

Don Hinrichsen

Don Hinrichsen is a senior consultant on population and environment for the United Nations Population Fund and the author of *Coastal Waters of the World: Trends, Threats, and Strategies*. In this viewpoint, Hinrichsen argues that in many countries the demand for food exceeds the available supply. The hunger caused by overpopulation, he argues, could be reduced by preventing unintended pregnancies through contraception. In his view, this would slow the growth in demand for food, giving governments more time to find ways to improve food production techniques.

As you read, consider the following questions:
1. How does the UN Food and Agriculture Organization define the term "food security," and, according to Hinrichsen, about how many people lack food security?
2. In the author's estimation, by what percentage would Asia have to increase its food production in order to feed the 5.4 billion people projected to live there by the year 2050?
3. According to Hinrichsen, what five constraints do developing nations face in trying to increase their food production?

Excerpted from "Winning the Food Race," by Don Hinrichsen, *Population Reports*, series M, no. 13. Baltimore, Johns Hopkins University School of Public Health, Population Information Program, November 1997. Reprinted with permission.

In poor countries, especially where population is growing rapidly, hunger and malnutrition are often critical problems. An estimated 2 billion people suffer from malnutrition and dietary deficiencies. More than 840 million people— disproportionately women and girl children—suffer chronic malnourishment. Each year about 18 million people, mostly children, die from starvation, malnutrition, and related causes.

The World Food Summit in 1996 focused international attention on the concept of *food security*—access by all people to "safe and nutritious food to maintain a healthy and active life," according to the UN Food and Agriculture Organization (FAO). Worrisome trends in agricultural production and current international trade policies raise questions about whether food production and distribution can improve fast enough to overtake population growth and reach the goal of food security.

Discouraging New Trends

From the 1960s until a few years ago, world food supply kept pace with population growth. New agricultural technologies, better seed varieties, and irrigation—the Green Revolution—expanded the food supply. At the same time, in many developing countries contraceptive use has risen substantially, and fertility has fallen rapidly, amounting to a reproductive revolution. Between 1985 and 1995, however, in 64 of 105 countries studied by the U.N. Food and Agriculture Organization (FAO), food production lagged behind population growth. Africa now produces nearly 30% less food per person than in 1967.

Moreover, trying to meet the rising demand for food is leading people to overuse the world's finite resource base. Most developing countries already are cultivating virtually all arable land. In some areas fertile soils are being exploited faster than they can regenerate. Fresh water supplies are becoming degraded or exhausted. Yields from capture fisheries have fallen. Such trends make it increasingly difficult to meet the world's food needs. . . .

Population Growth and Food Needs

In many developing countries rapid population growth makes it difficult for agricultural production to keep pace with the rising demand for food. Most developing countries already are cultivating virtually all arable land and are bringing ever more marginal land under cultivation.

"Unfortunately, population growth continues to outstrip food availability in many countries," reported Jacques Diouf, director-general of the United Nations Food and Agriculture Organization, at the 1996 World Food Summit in Rome. For example, between 1985 and 1995, food production lagged behind population growth in 64 of 105 developing countries studied by FAO. Among regions, Africa fared the worst. Food production per person fell in 31 of 46 African countries.

Concerns about lagging agricultural production and rapid population growth, as well as inadequate food distribution systems, have focused international attention on the concept of *food security*. FAO defines food security as a "state of affairs where all people at all times have access to safe and nutritious food to maintain a healthy and active life." By this definition about 2 billion people—one person in every three—lack food security. Either they cannot grow enough food themselves, or they cannot afford to purchase enough in the domestic marketplace. As a result, they suffer from micronutrient and protein energy deficiencies in their diets. . . .

Population: The Demand Side

Population growth, along with changes in people's living standards and dietary preferences, largely determine changes in the demand for food. Throughout history societies have raced to keep the food supply equal to or ahead of population growth. The race has not always been won, as the history of widespread malnutrition and famines attests.

Currently, world population is growing by over 80 million people a year—that is, by 1 billion people every 12 to 13 years. Such change is unprecedented. It was not until about 1800 that the world's total population reached 1 billion. It took approximately another century to reach 2 billion. In the past 50 years more people have been added to the world's population than during the previous 4 million years.

The world's population is expected to reach 6 billion in 1999. According to UN projections, by 2025 the world would contain over 8 billion people, of whom some 6.8 billion would live in developing countries.

Since the 1960s the rate of population growth has slowed. In what demographers have termed a reproductive revolution, fertility in developing countries has declined as contraceptive use has risen. Family planning programs have helped millions of couples avoid unintended pregnancies and thus have contributed importantly to reducing fertility rates. Because of family planning programs in the past, the world now contains 400 million fewer people than it would otherwise.

World population is growing by 1.5% per year today compared with 2% per year in the 1960s. In some developing countries, however, primarily in sub-Saharan Africa, population is still growing at 2% to 3.5% per year, rates at which populations would double in 20 to 35 years. Even growth rates of 2% or less create a powerful momentum for future population increase, particularly as they are applied to ever larger numbers of people. . . .

Food Production: The Supply Side

For most of the past 50 years food production has outpaced rising demand. World population has doubled since World War II, but food production has tripled. In the developing world the daily calories available per person increased from an average of 1,925 calories in 1961 to 2,540 in 1992. World food production has expanded since the early 1960s due mainly to the Green Revolution—adoption of crop rotation, the production and use of petroleum-based fertilizers and chemical pesticides, expanded irrigation, and the introduction of genetically superior, disease-resistant cultivars (cultivated crops).

The trend may now be changing for the worse, however. Since about 1990 global grain production has risen only slightly and, despite slower rates of population growth, grain supplies per capita have fallen. In the worst case, Africa now produces nearly 30% *less* food per person than it did in 1967. The reasons for the change in the trend include not only rapid population growth on the demand side, but also higher population densities in traditional agricultural areas, fragmentation of small farmsteads, poor land management, and inappropriate agricultural and economic policies, all of which suppress supply.

With one-third of world population lacking food security now, FAO estimates that world food production would have to double to provide food security for the 8 billion people projected for 2025. By 2050, when world population is projected to be over 9 billion, the situation would be even more challenging. At current levels of consumption, without allowing for additional imports of food, Africa would have to increase food production by 300% to provide minimally adequate diets for the 2 billion people projected in 2050; Latin America would have to increase food production by 80% to feed a projected 810 million people; and Asia's food production would have to grow by 70% to feed the 5.4 billion people projected. Even North America would have to increase food production by 30% to feed a projected 384 million people in 2050.

Rapid population growth not only pushes up demand for food but may also be starting to diminish supply as well. As people try to obtain higher yields from heavily used natural resources, soil loss worsens, fresh water becomes scarcer, and pollution increases. As a result the developing world's capacity to expand food production may well be shrinking, not expanding. . . .

While food is abundant in many areas, millions of people in developing countries are undernourished. Each year about 18 million people, mostly children, die from starvation, malnutrition, and related causes. An estimated 2 billion people suffer from malnutrition and dietary deficiencies; some 840 million of them are chronically malnourished. In sub-Saharan Africa as many as 70% of all women are anemic.

About 200 million children under age five—40% of all children of this age in the developing world—lack sufficient nutrition to lead fully active lives. One indicator of chronic malnutrition among children is the percentage who are stunted—that is, short for their age compared with international standards set by the World Health Organization (WHO). Stunting among children ages 3 months to 3 years varies widely among countries, but at least one child in every three was stunted in over 40% of countries surveyed by the Demographic and Health Surveys between 1987 and 1996.

Recent projections by the International Food Policy Research Institute (IFPRI) indicate that child hunger and malnutrition are not likely to be reduced much over the course of the next several decades. According to IFPRI, 150 million children under the age of six will still be malnourished in 2020, just 20% fewer than in 1993. In Africa the number of malnourished children is expected to increase by 45% between 1993 and 2020, reaching 40 million. . . .

Be fruitful and multiply...

Now, divide.

Clay Bennett/North American Syndicate. Reprinted with permission.

Since the early 1980s FAO has issued yearly reports listing the world's low-income, food-deficit countries. In 1996 there were 82 such countries, half of them in Africa. By definition, these countries have a per capita gross national product (GNP) of US$1,345 or less and have had a net deficit in grain trade over the preceding five years.

The situation could grow worse for food-deficit countries. In many of them, population growth is among the most rapid in the world, and most face serious constraints to increasing agricultural production. To one degree or another, these constraints affect many other developing countries as well:

- *Limited agricultural land.* The best agricultural land is already being cultivated. Most of the remaining potential agricultural land consists of clay or sandy soils, often on steep slopes with limited water supplies, or nutrient-poor tropical soils;
- *Limited water supplies.* Fresh water resources are scarce, and there often are severe water shortages during dry seasons;
- *Poverty.* Farmers often lack enough land to feed their families, let alone to produce food surpluses for sale, while their countries cannot afford to import enough food to meet people's needs;
- *Poor access to credit.* Many farmers cannot obtain loans to bridge the gap in their incomes between harvests and must seek work as laborers or even sell off some of their land to survive;
- *Lack of appropriate policies.* To produce more food, communities need help obtaining suitable technologies and crop varieties and developing sound agricultural strategies. . . .

Steps Toward Food Security

Achieving food security over the long term depends partly on slowing population growth. Providing family planning to all couples who want it would go far to reducing fertility rates and slowing population growth in many developing countries. An estimated 100 million married women, and probably millions of other women, are interested in avoiding pregnancy but are not currently using contraception.

At the same time, a second Green Revolution could increase yields and buy more time for world population eventually to stabilize. In this revolution practicing sustainable agriculture—that is, protecting natural resources from becoming increasingly degraded and polluted—will be essential. Also, developing countries can explore new ways to help meet their food needs. These include improving yields on marginal land, farming forests, expanding aquaculture, rediscovering forgotten foods, and encouraging urban agriculture. . . .

Winning the food race is likely to require decades of effort at international, national, and local levels. It will require cooperation among policies and programs in agriculture, resource management, health care including family planning, and economic development. In any strategy, reaching replacement-level fertility as quickly as possible provides a needed foundation. Particularly for the more than 80 low-income food-deficit countries, slowing population growth could buy more time to address the needs of farmers, improve living conditions, and raise agricultural productivity, while helping to protect the soil and water resources needed for food production in the future.

"The human population could be halved, quartered, decimated even, yet hunger would still remain. So long as one person has the power to deny food to another, even two people may be judged 'too many.'"

Overpopulation Is Not the Main Cause of World Hunger

Nicholas Hildyard

Nicholas Hildyard, formerly on the editorial staff of the *Ecologist*, is now with the Cornerhouse, a research organization in New York City. In the following viewpoint, Hildyard argues that the main culprit in perpetuating hunger on the planet is not the growing population but the market forces that deliberately induce food scarcity in order to keep the production and distribution of food crops profitable. In his view, landowners interested only in profit also typically ignore the ecological damage that agricultural practices often cause; this undermines the capacity of the land to produce food, and further exacerbates worldwide hunger.

As you read, consider the following questions:
1. In the author's opinion, what forces help prevent starvation in commons-based regimes, and what forces contribute to food scarcity in market-based regimes?
2. According to Hildyard, what percentage of farm owners own half the farmland in the United States?
3. According to the author, how many people currently experience socially induced food scarcity?

Excerpted from Nicholas Hildyard, "Too Many for What? The Social Generation of Food 'Scarcity' and 'Overpopulation,'" published by The Corner House, Sturminster Newton Dorset DT10 IYJ, England, as it appeared in *The Ecologist*, November/December 1996. Reprinted with permission of the author.

Globe, Inc. is "overpopulated". And as long as access to food and other resources is determined by inequitable power relationships, it will remain so. Because no matter how much food is produced, how few babies are born or how dramatically human numbers fall, it is the nature of the modern market economy remorselessly to generate "scarcity". Blaming such socially-generated scarcity and ecological degradation on "overpopulation" or "underproduction" has long provided the more powerful with an explanation for human misery that does not indict themselves and that legitimizes various ideologies of exclusion. Without changes in the social and economic relationships that currently determine the production, distribution and consumption of food in the world, there will always be those who are judged "surplus to requirements" and who are thus excluded from the wherewithal to live. The human population could be halved, quartered, decimated even, yet hunger would still remain. So long as one person has the power to deny food to another, even two people may be judged "too many".

Recognizing the existence of socially-generated scarcity—insufficient necessities for some people and not others—is not to deny *absolute* scarcity—insufficient resources, no matter how equitably they are distributed. We live on a finite planet and there are, incontrovertibly, limits to the ability of the earth to accommodate human numbers, pollution, resource depletion and other demands on its "ecological services". It is, however, to insist that differentiating between socially-generated scarcity and absolute scarcity is a *sine qua non* for any sensible discussion of the causes of food insecurity.

The Experience of Scarcity

Scarcity—in the sense of a dearth of food or other necessities—is not a new phenomenon. Throughout history, communities have had to contend with failed harvests or disturbances such as war which have led to food insufficiencies. But not everyone experiences this scarcity in the same way: who gets to eat and who goes hungry during periods of insufficiency has always depended on the ability of households and individuals to gain access to food, and hence on the distribution of economic and political power within a community and the wider society.

In commons-based regimes, where the management of land is a community affair, scarcity and its resulting hardship tend to be a shared phenomenon because the survival of all depends upon no one putting any one else in the community at risk. Working the land, for example, tends to be a co-operative business, with richer farmers just as bound by reciprocal labour arrangements as poorer farmers. Likewise, the joint management of water and other resources means that farmers are under intense social pressure to respect the rights of each other if their own rights are to be respected. The commons culture of joint "ownership" and responsibilities therefore limits the ability of any one group or individual to exercise institutional power over others. This does not mean that everyone is equal in the commons: gender, class and caste inequalities, for instance, certainly exist, both between households and within households. In general, however, a rough equity prevails in which everyone has some degree of bargaining power. Thus no one is likely to starve whilst others are comfortable.

In market-based regimes, people's experience of scarcity is very different. In an undiluted market economy, access to food is no longer dependent on being part of—and contributing to—a social network: instead, food goes to those who have the money to buy it. Only those who, in the economists' jargon, have the income to translate their biological needs into "effective demand" get to eat. In today's global supermarket, people earning $25 a year—if they are lucky—must compete for the same food with people who earn $25 an hour, or even $25 a minute.

It is this market logic—and the power structures that drive it—that lies behind the paradox of people starving despite abundant local harvests; that explains why shiploads of grain were exported daily from the famine-stricken Horn of Africa during the 1980s to feed already well-fed Europeans; that ensures that cats and dogs belonging to European pet owners can be better fed than children of low-paid or unemployed European workers; that condemns an estimated 800 million people (including two million children in the UK alone) to malnutrition and hunger; and that ensures that, for many people, the experience of scarcity—insufficient food—is not a *temporary* phenomenon. Nor, as was typically the case in commons regimes, is it a phenomenon more or less shared by all; it has become a perennial feature of life for an increasing number of people.

The deliberate manufacture of scarcity now provides one of the principal means through which state and private interests "monopolize resources, control markets and suppress the demographic majority". Such use of scarcity as an instrument of "population control"—in its sense of "controlling people"—is not unique to free market economies or to any one historical era. It is, however, only possible in societies where elite interests—whether state apparatchiks, feudal landlords, colonial sahibs, military wannabes or corporate executives—have managed, more or less, to deny the majority of people control over the resources and markets on which their livelihoods depend.

Generating Scarcity of Land

Historically, control over land has always been vital to the livelihoods of the world's poorest people. Lack of access to land not only denies people the ability to grow or to gather their own food; it also excludes them from a source of power. Who controls the land—and how they do so—affects how land is used and to whom the benefits for its use accrue.

Highly-concentrated land ownership is now a feature of agriculture in both North and South. In the US, nearly half the country's farmland is held by just 124,000 corporations or individuals—just four per cent of the total number of farm owners. In Guatemala, 65 percent of the best agricultural land is owned by just two per cent of the population—a figure that is not atypical for other countries in Central America. In Brazil, a mere 340 of the largest landowners, many of whom are foreign-owned transnational companies, own more land than all the country's peasants put together. The 18 largest landowners own an area equivalent to that of The Netherlands, Portugal and Switzerland combined. In the Philippines, five per cent of all families control 80 per cent of the agricultural land, despite seven land reform laws since 1933.

The corollary of such concentration of land ownership in

the hands of the few is land scarcity for the many. In the Philippines, about 72 per cent of rural households (three-fifths of the Philippine population) are landless or near-landless. Tenant farmers must contend with rents which account for between 25 and 90 per cent of their production costs. Usury at rates of 100 per cent in three months or 50 per cent in one month is common. Half of all those who make a living from agriculture are farm workers, often earning as little as $1 a day.

In Central America as a whole, small and medium-sized farms producing for local consumption and local sale represent about 94 per cent of existing farms but use only 9 per cent of the farmland. Meanwhile, 85 per cent of the best farmland is used to grow crops for export. . . .

Modernization and Scarcity

Land concentration in the Third World is not accidental. It has always been fiercely resisted, not least by popular movements demanding land redistribution. Imbalances of power, however, have enabled landowners to ensure that, by and large, land reform programmes have either been put on hold, subverted or short-lived. In other instances, they have been framed, not as a means of addressing insecurity of tenure, but as a means of replacing peasant systems of farming with industrialized agriculture.

By defining rural poverty in terms of insufficient productivity (*solution:* high-yielding crop varieties and agrochemicals) rather than a lack of access to sufficient land (*solution:* agrarian reform), some governments, in alliance with richer farmers and international development agencies, used "land reform" to appropriate land for the Green Revolution instead of freeing it up for peasant agriculture. The ultimate aim of such "reforms" was to transform Third World farming into "a dynamic productive sector" by extending export crop production and by drawing peasants still further into the cash economy where they were at a disadvantage.

The promotion of off-farm inputs—chemical fertilizers, pesticides and improved seeds—has forced farmers to buy what was previously free, in addition to locking them into a cycle of diminishing returns on fertilizers and increasing pesticide use. As a result, thousands of small farmers—including those who had gained land under previous land reform programmes—have fallen into debt and their land holdings bought up by richer neighbours. In South Korea, where the army was mobilized to rip up traditional varieties of rice and to compel farmers to plant Green Revolution varieties, the number of rural households in debt rose "from 76 per cent in 1971 to 90 per cent in 1983 and to an astounding 98 per cent in 1985." As a result, farmers have left the land in droves: 34,000 migrated to the cities in 1986, 41,000 in 1987 and 50,000 in 1988. Many of the farmers who remain have now abandoned the new varieties and are returning to planting traditional seeds.

The Myth That There Are Too Many Mouths to Feed

Although rapid population growth remains a serious concern in many countries, nowhere does population density explain hunger. For every Bangladesh, a densely populated and hungry country, we find a Nigeria, Brazil or Bolivia, where abundant food resources coexist with hunger. Costa Rica, with only half of Honduras' cropped acres per person, boasts a life expectancy—one indicator of nutrition—11 years longer than that of Honduras and close to that of developed countries.

Rapid population growth is not the root cause of hunger. Like hunger itself, it results from underlying inequities that deprive people, especially poor women, of economic opportunity and security. Rapid population growth and hunger are endemic to societies where land ownership, jobs, education, health care, and old age security are beyond the reach of most people. Those Third World societies with dramatically successful early and rapid reductions of population growth rates—China, Sri Lanka, Colombia, Cuba and the Indian state of Kerala—prove that the lives of the poor, especially poor women, must improve before they can choose to have fewer children.

Food First Institute for Food and Development Policy, *12 Myths About Hunger*, 1998.

Thus, for marginal groups of people, the promotion of Green Revolution technologies—the hallmark of "efficient" farming—has generated yet more scarcity of land and of food as the land becomes further concentrated in fewer and fewer hands. . . .

Scarcity and the Market

As land and water become increasingly degraded, and control over such resources increasingly concentrated, so the livelihoods of peasant farmers, the landless and the near-landless become increasingly precarious. No longer able to rely on growing their food, the vast majority have to buy their food. How much and what they get to eat depends on their ability to earn money or on the state's willingness to support them. . . .

Eight hundred million people now experience socially-induced food scarcity. Rather than address the inequitable power relations that lie behind such scarcity, however, "solutions" that minimize disruption to the status quo are put forward by the generators of such scarcity. . . .

In the absence of radical change to current economic and social structures, however, increased output—whatever way it is achieved—will not translate into increased numbers of people fed. In a world in which scarcity is continually generated as an unavoidable—some would argue, deliberate—feature of the food system, the experience of hunger will only increase.

In addition, by inexorably undermining the capacity of land to produce food, the ecological damage caused by intensive farming is creating the conditions for absolute scarcity—where even equitable economic and social arrangements may prove insufficient to prevent widespread human impoverishment. Artificial fertilizers and chemical sprays, for example, have disastrously undermined the natural fertility of soils. As farmers have ceased to apply manure and other organic material to the land, so the soil's structure in many areas has begun to break down, increasing its vulnerability to erosion—an estimated 24 billion tonnes of soil being eroded from the world's agricultural lands every year. This is enough soil to fill a train of freight cars stretching from the Earth to the Moon—and back again—five times.

In arid areas, the introduction of perennial irrigation has brought the added problem of salinization. Irrigation agriculture is one of the most productive forms of farming, but the irrigation of poorly drained land, year after year, has waterlogged the soils, causing salts in the groundwater to rise to the surface, where they accumulate, turning vast stretches of farmland into salt-encrusted desert. In many areas, irrigated land is now so severely degraded that it is unfit for agriculture. . . .

Two Too Many

Discussions of population and food supply which leave out power relations will always mask the true nature of food scarcity—who gets to eat and who doesn't—and lead to "solutions" that are simplistic, technocratic, frequently oppressive and gender-blind—all of which, ultimately, reinforce the very structures that create ecological damage and hunger. To reiterate: so long as one person has the power to deny food to another, even two people may be judged "too many". Recognizing that fact—and putting equity at the centre of the debate—is a *sine qua non* for any sensible discussion of the causes of food insecurity and food scarcity.

"As a species, we already are well in the midst of a major bio-geophysical transformation of the Earth."

Overpopulation Could Lead to Extinction

Timothy C. Weiskel

Timothy C. Weiskel, associate director of the Pacific Rim Research Center at Harvard University, asserts in the following viewpoint that the geometric growth of the human population is responsible for an unprecedented extinction of other species of flora and fauna and a general degradation of the planet's biodiversity. If countermeasures are not taken immediately, Weiskel argues, the continued decimation of the earth's resources could lead to starvation, war, and even the extinction of mankind.

As you read, consider the following questions:

1. In the author's view, what are the two important differences that exist between the present "extinction event" and the one that resulted in the demise of the dinosaurs?
2. According to Weiskel, why have humans remained ignorant of, and indifferent to, the fate of other species?
3. How, in Weiskel's opinion, have advances in technology fueled the growth of human population?

Excerpted from "Can Humanity Survive Unrestricted Population Growth?" by Timothy C. Weiskel, *USA Today*, January 1995. Reprinted with permission from *USA Today* magazine.

Biologists are reassuring that the invertebrates and microbial species are likely to survive the current epoch relatively unscathed. This message provides small comfort when one begins to realize that the larger point is that life as we know it is undergoing massive extinction. More precisely, geologists, evolutionary biologists, and paleontologists are reporting evidence in their professional journals that the planet currently is in the midst of a global "extinction event" that equals or exceeds in scale those catastrophic episodes in the geological record which marked the end of the dinosaurs and numerous other species.

At least two important differences exist between this extinction episode and those previously documented. First, in earlier events of similar magnitude, the question of agency and the sequence of species extinctions have remained largely a mystery. In the current extinction event, however, scientists know with a high degree of certainty what the effective agent of system-wide collapse is and have a fairly good notion of the specific dynamics and sequence of these extinctions.

Second, previous events of this nature seem to have involved extraterrestrial phenomena, such as episodic meteor collisions. Alternatively, the long-term flux of incoming solar radiation that results from the harmonic convergence of the Earth's asymmetrical path around the sun and the "wobble" on its axis also drives system-wide changes generating periodic advances and retreats of continental ice sheets in high latitudes. These, too, cause system-wide transformations and have precipitated extinction events in the past.

Human-Caused Extinctions

In contrast to these extraterrestrial or celestial phenomena that served as the forcing functions behind previous mass extinctions, the current event results from an internally generated dynamic. The relatively stable exchanges among various biotic communities have shifted in a short period of time into an unstable phase of runaway, exponential growth for a small subset of the species mix—human beings, their biological symbionts (organisms living in a cooperative relationship), and their associates.

The seemingly unrestrained growth of these populations

has unleashed a pattern of accentuated parasitism and predation upon a selected number of proximate species that were deemed by them to be useful. This accentuated parasitism led to the creation of human-influenced biological environments. These, in turn, drove hundreds of other species directly into extinction—sometimes within periods of only a few centuries or decades. More significantly, this pattern of unrestrained growth and subsequent collapse has repeated itself again and again, engendering in each instance a syndrome of generalized habitat destruction. Over time, it has precipitated the cumulative extinction of thousands of species as one civilization after another has devastated its environment and dispersed its remnant populations far afield in search of new resources that it can plunder and squander.

For a variety of reasons—some of them apparently related to their religious beliefs—humans remain fundamentally ignorant of or collectively indifferent toward the fate of their fellow species, insisting instead that measurements of human welfare should be the only criteria for governing human behavior. Apparently, the right to life is effectively defined as the "right to human life." This anthropocentric belief in human exceptionalism has characterized past civilizations and remains no less dominant today. The most pervasive form of this religiously held belief in modern times is techno-scientific salvationism. Scientists and baby boomers alike promise us that technological miracles will save us from our rapidly deteriorating ecological circumstance and that no substantial sacrifice will be required. After all, "thanks to science," there are miracle crops, miracle drugs, and Miracle Whip! What more could be needed?

The Population Explosion

The fact is, we must have a great deal more to survive as a society and a species. In reality, the true immensity of the problem is just beginning to be recognized. Consider, for instance, the truly dramatic dimensions of humans' recent growth as a species. By recent, I mean in evolutionary terms and in terms of the relatively long time scales required to engineer stable social adjustment to changing circumstances. In evolutionary terms, it took from the dawn of humanity to roughly 1945 for the human species to reach a population of about 2,000,000,000. That figure has more than doubled—indeed, nearly tripled—since 1945. Experts say that figure well could reach a total of 9,000,000,000 during the rest of our lifetimes if left to grow at projected rates.

Consider, as well, the over-all ecological "footprint" of human expansion over the millennia, particularly as humans have come to congregate in cities. Depending upon how one wishes to segment humans from their biological relatives, humans have been around for roughly 1,000,000 years. It is only in the last 1.2% of that history—roughly the last 12,000 years—that people have come to depend upon agriculture, and only the last 6,000 years or so that they have begun to transform settlement patterns into urban concentrations.

We are still in the midst of what might be called the "urban transition" in the human evolutionary experiment. It is not clear that the transition will be achieved successfully or that the human bio-evolutionary experiment will endure very much longer in evolutionary terms. Nevertheless, there is enough evidence available about the urban transition in human history to begin generating some general statements.

Population Growth Leads to Warfare and Ecological Disaster

The evidence of environmental archaeologists is especially sobering in this context. The history of cities has been associated with that of repeated ecological disaster. Their growth has engendered rapid regional deforestation, the depletion of ground-water aquifers, accelerated soil erosion, plant genetic simplification, periodic outbreaks of disease among pest species and domesticated animals, large-scale human malnutrition, and the development and spread of epidemics. In many cases, the individual elements of ecological decline have been linked in positive feedback processes that reinforced one another and led to precipitous collapse of particular cities.

To overcome the limitations imposed by these patterns of localized environmental collapse, cities historically have sought to dominate rural regions in their immediate vicinity and extend links of trade and alliance to similarly constituted cities further afield. As arable land and strategic water supplies became more scarce and more highly valued, violent conflict between individual city-states emerged, leading in short succession to the development of leagues of allied cities and subsequently to the formation of kingdoms and empires with organized armies for conquest and permanent defense.

The 20 Most Populous Countries, Now and in 2050

1998			2050	
Rank	Country	Population in millions	Country	Population in millions
1	China 1,255		India 1,533	
2	India 976		China 1,517	
3	United States . . .274		Pakistan 357	
4	Indonesia 207		United States . . .348	
5	Brazil 165		Nigeria 339	
6	Pakistan 148		Indonesia 318	
7	Russia 147		Brazil 243	
8	Japan 126		Bangladesh 218	
9	Bangladesh 124		Ethiopia 213	
10	Nigeria 122		Iran 170	
11	Mexico 96		The Congo 165	
12	Germany 82		Mexico 154	
13	Vietnam 78		Philippines 131	
14	Iran 73		Vietnam 130	
15	Philippines 72		Egypt 115	
16	Egypt 66		Russia 114	
17	Turkey 64		Japan 110	
18	Ethiopia 62		Turkey 98	
19	Thailand 60		South Africa 91	
20	France 59		Tanzania 89	

United Nations, *World Population Prospects: The 1996 Revision.*

Even with the limitations of pre-industrial technology, the results of these conflicts could be devastating to local or regional ecosystems, particularly when victorious groups sought to destroy the ecological viability of defeated groups with such policies as scorched-earth punishment and the sowing of salt over the arable land in defeated territory. The environmental impact of warfare and the preparation for battle has been devastating in all ages. Author C.S. Lewis' observation has proved sadly correct that "the so-called struggle of man against nature is really a struggle of man against man with nature as an instrument."

Human Populations Tend to Expand and Collapse

Demographic historians have added further details to the picture of repeated ecological disaster painted by environmental archaeologists. Human populations have demonstrated again and again the long-term regional tendency to expand and collapse. These undulating patterns are referred to by demographers as the "millennial long waves" (MLW), and they appear to be manifest in both the Old World and the New.

Two patterns are discernible across all cases despite the considerable differences between regions. First, the human population is both highly unstable and highly resilient. There is considerable variation in the amplitude of the population waves; therefore, human populations can not be considered stable in regional terms. Moreover, the population is resilient in the sense that it bounces back from demographic catastrophe with an even stronger surge in reproductive performance. The second phenomena of the MLW on the regional level is that the frequency between their occurrence is shortened successively. Thus, populations seem to be collapsing and rebounding at higher and higher levels more and more frequently as we approach the present.

When we move beyond the regional evidence to a global scale, another important pattern emerges. Human populations seem to expand in spurts, corresponding to the quantities of energy they are able to harness with their available technology. This may emerge as a new way of stating the Malthusian theory of population limit. Economist Thomas Malthus focused on the relation of populations to their food supply, pointing out that, while populations tend to grow exponentially, the food supply tends to grow only arithmetically. As a result, populations ultimately are limited, as their reproductive performance outstrips the food supply needed to keep them alive and there are periodic widespread famines.

Since Malthus, people have come to realize that "food" itself is really a form of captured solar energy that humans can assimilate to maintain themselves and do work. If this observation is built upon to reformulate Malthus' observation in terms of energy instead of food itself, we are probably close to a broad-level truth about the human species. Simply put, the Malthusian law can be restated in these terms: Human populations tend to expand to the levels supported by the supplies of energy that they can mobilize with available technology.

The industrial era in world history marks an unprecedented period in human evolution history from this perspective. Never before have global populations experienced such high rates of growth for such sustained duration, reaching a worldwide climax with an average annual population increase of two percent during the decade from 1965 to 1975. Demographic historian Paul Demeny has described this extraordinary period quite succinctly:

"It took countless millennia to reach a global 1700 population of somewhat under 700,000,000. The next 150 years, a tiny fraction of humankind's total history, roughly matched this performance. By 1950, global human numbers doubled again to surpass 2,500,000,000. The average annual rate of population growth was 0.34% in the 18th century; it climbed to 0.54% in the 19th century and to 0.84% in the first half of the 20th. In absolute terms, the first five decades following 1700 added 90,000,000 to global numbers. Between 1900 and 1950, not withstanding two world wars, an influenza pandemic, and a protracted global economic crisis, the net addition to population size amounted to nearly 10 times that much."

As Demeny summarized the situation: "Clearly, viewed in an evolutionary perspective, the 250 years between 1700 and 1950 have witnessed extraordinary success of the human species in terms of expanding numbers, a success that invokes the image of swarming." For demographic historians, then, it would seem that humans in the modern era are behaving much like a plague of locusts.

What is even more striking is that the pattern of distribution of this burgeoning population is one of rapid relocation into massive urban agglomerations. In 1700, less than 10% of the total world population of 700,000,000 lived in cities.

By 1950, 30% did. In North America, the urban proportion of the population had reached 64% by that time, while in Europe, it was 56%.

In 1700, only five cities had populations of 500,000 people. By 1900, that number had risen to 43. Of those, 16 had populations over 1,000,000. By now, however—in a span of less than 100 years—there are nearly 400 cities that exceed 1,000,000, and there soon will be scores of "megacities" with populations in excess of 10,000,000 people, particularly in the Pacific Rim.

Will Humanity Survive the Overpopulation Crisis?

Accordingly, it is clear that we can not avoid the problem. We have no choice. As a species, we already are well in the midst of a major bio-geophysical transformation of the Earth.

Can we survive it? Techno-boomers will assure us that of course we can. All we need is adequate incentives for investment, a sense of determination, inventiveness, and political will to make the "tough" decisions.

This well may be true, but it is essentially beside the point. The far more interesting question is: Will we survive it? Not just theoretically can we, but, in a very practical sense, will we? This only can be answered by looking carefully at what is meant by "we" and "survive." Techno-scientific salvationists—like other fundamentalists—are silent and often sadly ignorant of the social dimensions of the changes required to answer this larger set of questions.

Personally, I am not optimistic, but I remain hopeful that our political leaders will recognize that techno-scientific salvationism alone can not sustain us, especially since such a strategy to address our problems is likely to lead in the future, as it has in the past, to a growing gap between the "haves" and the "have nots." An increasingly divided human community will degrade the global environment further as factions within it struggle to dominate each other and exploit what remains of nature's resources. Political leaders must realize instead that we will need to build a compassionate sense of human community on a world scale to match the global environmental crisis that confronts everyone.

"People create resources. They bring into the world their time, effort, and ingenuity."

Overpopulation Is Not a Serious Problem

N. Gregory Mankiw

N. Gregory Mankiw, an economics professor at Harvard University and the author of *Principle of Economics*, argues in the following viewpoint that the increasing global population does not present a major threat to mankind or to the environment. On the contrary, Mankiw maintains, an increasing population is a blessing, since a larger number of people will come up with proportionately more ideas for making the world a better place.

As you read, consider the following questions:

1. In Mankiw's words, what is the reason for the increase in living standards over the past two centuries?
2. In the author's view, what is the "simple insight" shared by people who fear overpopulation, and what is the simple rebuttal to their arguments?
3. According to Mankiw, what solution does Bill McKibben offer for the problem of global warming, and what is a more direct solution?

Excerpted from "Be Fruitful and Multiply," by N. Gregory Mankiw, *Fortune*, September 7, 1998. Copyright ©1998 by Time Inc. Reprinted by permission of Time Inc.

I confess: My wife and I are about to commit what some people consider a socially irresponsible act. Toward the end of the summer, we will bring our third child into the world.

A third child means, of course, that my wife and I are contributing to the world's population explosion, and to some people this makes our decision more than personal. To see how guilty I should feel, I just read the recent book by nature writer Bill McKibben, *Maybe One: A Personal and Environmental Argument for Single-Child Families.* McKibben tries to accomplish through persuasion what China has done through government fiat—make one child per couple the norm. The book wasn't published in time to change my family size, but even if it had been, it wouldn't have persuaded me to abstain from reproduction.

An Old and Erroneous Argument

As McKibben is well aware, fear of overpopulation has a long and embarrassing history. Two centuries ago, Thomas Malthus argued that an ever-increasing population would continually strain society's ability to produce goods and services. As a result, mankind was doomed to forever live in poverty—a prediction that led Thomas Carlyle to label economics "the dismal science."

Fortunately, Malthus was far off the mark. Although the world population has increased about sixfold over the past two centuries, living standards are much higher. The reason is that growth in mankind's ingenuity has far exceeded growth in population. New ideas about how to produce and even about the kinds of goods to produce have led to greater prosperity than Malthus—or anyone else of his era—could have ever imagined.

The failure of Malthus' prediction, however, has not stopped others from repeating it. The most famous modern Malthusian is biologist Paul Ehrlich, whose 1968 book, *The Population Bomb*, warned of impending worldwide shortages in food and natural resources. Thirty years later, however, most natural resources are in abundant supply and are available at low prices. Even the famines that sometimes ravage less-developed countries are rarely due to overpopulation—civil war is a more common cause. Nonetheless, the fear of worldwide shortages because of overpopulation remains widespread.

Among the wealthy, reducing population growth is a popular cause. When David Packard, co-founder of Hewlett-Packard and father of four, died leaving $9 billion to his foundation, he specified that the foundation's highest priority should be lowering global birth rates. Packard's efforts may someday be dwarfed by those of investor Warren Buffett, father of three. Buffett claims he will give away most of his vast wealth, and according to some reports, the problem that most moves Buffett is the population explosion.

Reprinted with permission from Chuck Asay and Creator's Syndicate.

Those who fear overpopulation share a simple insight: People use resources. They eat food, drive cars, and take up space. Because resources are scarce, the only way to improve living standards, Malthusians argue, is to limit the number of people with whom we have to share these resources.

Humans Are Society's Most Important Resource

The rebuttal to this argument is equally simple: People create resources. They bring into the world their time, effort, and ingenuity. Before deciding whether world population growth is a curse or a blessing, we have to ask ourselves whether an extra person added to the planet uses more or less resources than he or she creates.

Environmentalists such as McKibben view humans as rapacious consumers who devour as much as they can get their hands on. About this, the environmentalists are largely right. But there is no problem as long as people pay for what they consume. In a market economy, the price system ensures that no one can consume resources without first creating some of equal or greater value.

Problems do arise when important resources fail to have prices attached to them. For instance, consider the issue that most concerns McKibben—global warming caused by the use of fossil fuels. Because people burning gasoline in their cars or oil in their furnaces do not pay for their impact on climate, they burn too much. The solution, according to McKibben, is fewer people. A more direct solution is a tax on fossil fuels.

Perhaps the most important resource without a price is society's pool of ideas. Every time a baby is born, there is some chance that he or she will be the next Newton, Darwin, or Einstein. And when that happens, everyone benefits. Although the government can easily protect the environment with a well-designed tax system, spurring the production of great ideas is much harder. The best way to get more geniuses is to have more people.

As a serial procreator, therefore, I make no apologies. When I welcome Peter Mankiw onto our planet, I will do so without a shred of guilt. I don't guarantee that he will find a cure for cancer or a solution to global warming, but there is always a chance. And in that chance lies the hope for our species.

Periodical Bibliography

The following articles have been selected to supplement the diverse views presented in this chapter. Addresses are provided for periodicals not indexed in the *Readers' Guide to Periodical Literature*, the *Alternative Press Index*, the *Social Sciences Index*, or the *Index to Legal Periodicals and Books*.

Virginia Abernathy	"Population Explosion Triggered by Wealth," *Forum for Applied Research and Public Policy*, Summer 1997.
Kenneth Arrow	"Economic Growth, Carrying Capacity, and the Environment," *Science*, April 1995.
Peter T. Bauer	"Population Growth: Disaster or Blessing?" *Independent Review*, Summer 1998.
William Bender and Margaret Smith	"Population, Food, and Nutrition," *Population Bulletin*, February 1997.
Lester Brown	"The Numbers Don't Lie: Why Malthus Was Right," *Free Inquiry*, Spring 1999.
Lester Brown and Brian Halweil	"China's Water Shortage Could Shake World Food Security," *Worldwatch*, July/August 1998.
Roy W. Brown	"When We 'Hit the Wall,'" *Free Inquiry*, Spring 1999.
Margaret Catley-Carlson and Judith A.M. Outlaw	"Poverty and Population Issues: Clarifying the Connections," *Journal of International Affairs*, Fall 1998.
Joel E. Cohen	"Population Growth and Earth's Human Carrying Capacity," *Science*, July 21, 1995.
Mary H. Cooper	"Population and the Environment: The Issues," *CQ Researcher*, July 17, 1998.
Partha Dasgupta	"The Population Problem: Theory and Evidence," *Journal of Economic Literature*, December 1995.
J.P. Davidson	"World Population and Your Life," *Vital Speeches of the Day*, June 15, 1995.
Gregg Easterbrook	"Measuring American Society: Malthus and His Disciples Were Simply Wrong," *Public Perspective*, June 1995.
Robert Livernash and Eric Rodenburg	"Population Change, Resources, and the Environment," *Population Bulletin*, March 1998.
David Pimentel, Xuewen Huang, Ana Cordova, and Marcia Pimentel	"Impact of Population Growth on Food Supplies and Environment," *Population and Environment*, September 1997.

Can Nations Control Population Without Violating Individuals' Reproductive Freedom?

Chapter Preface

Many nations have set out to control their populations. Some have adopted pronatalist policies that offer incentives for having large families. More commonly, nations have adopted antinatalist policies to decrease their population. Most population control advocates aim for zero population growth (ZPG), under which the average couple has two children (replacement fertility). This results in no net population growth.

More restrictive population policies call for negative population growth (NPG). In China, for example, each couple is permitted to have only one child. Although it is considered coercive by many, the policy has not met with any organized opposition by the Chinese people. It may be that the Chinese have accepted the one-child policy, while many in the West find it objectionable, because of cultural differences.

Population is affected by much more than just whether the government provides incentives or disincentives for having children. The choices people make about how many children they have are influenced by family, friends, tradition, and religious beliefs. Many of the issues associated with population control, such as whether abortion should be legal, are more controversial in some cultures than they are in others.

One major question associated with population control is whether or not people have a fundamental right to have children. Should there be globally recognized human rights that protect an individual's reproductive choices? Are reproductive, health, and sexual rights legitimate human rights? Some say yes, and argue that China's one-child policy constitutes a grave human rights violation. Population control advocates, on the other hand, argue that reproductive choices should not be left solely to individuals because of the highly destructive consequences of overpopulation.

The authors in the following chapter will debate what principles should guide population policies, and whether reproductive decisions should be left entirely to the individual or whether government, religion, and other institutions have a role to play in the choices people make about having children.

> *"In the developing world, at least 120
> million married women and a large but
> undefined number of unmarried women
> want more control over their pregnancies,
> but cannot get family planning services."*

Contraception and Abortion Are Necessary to Control Population

John M. Swomley

John M. Swomley is a professor of social ethics at the St. Paul School of Theology, president of Americans for Religious Liberty, and vice president of the American Civil Liberties Union. Swomley believes that overpopulation could be controlled in developing nations if their governments promoted the use of contraception and made abortion legal, safe, and accessible. He maintains that the primary opposition to these population control efforts is the Catholic Church, which forbids the use of contraception and abortion.

As you read, consider the following questions:

1. Approximately how many migrant refugees were there in 1995, according to Swomley?
2. Of the roughly 2 billion people that make up the global workforce, approximately how many does Swomley say are unemployed or underemployed?
3. What is *National Catholic Reporter* editor Tom Fox's view of the Catholic Church's opposition to birth control, as quoted by the author?

Excerpted from "The Population Wars," by John M. Swomley, *The Humanist*, July/August 1998. Reprinted with permission from the author.

Since the end of the Cold War, the nature of war has changed. No longer are we fighting other countries but, rather, ourselves. According to the United Nations, only three of the world's eighty-two armed conflicts in 1989 through 1992 were between countries; the rest were within countries. They have been the result of our failure to prevent reactionary religious forces from limiting and, at times, destroying the opportunity of millions worldwide to receive family planning, birth control, and legal abortion services.

In its 1997 quadrennial *Defense Review*, the Pentagon warns of a pending catastrophe:

> Some governments will lose their ability to maintain public order and provide for the needs of their people, creating the conditions for civil unrest, famine, [and] massive flows of migrants across international borders. . . . Uncontrolled flows of migrants will sporadically destabilize regions of the world and threaten American interests and citizens.

Refugees from the Population Wars

We are now witnessing these massive flows of economic refugees from poverty-stricken countries and other refugees from the population wars. According to the U.N. high commissioner of refugees, there were 27.4 million migrant refugees in the world in 1995. This is 4.4 million higher than the year before and 17 million more than the preceding ten years. Another 20 million people were refugees within their own countries.

The war in Rwanda, which has resulted in 1.8 million refugees living outside Rwanda's borders in 1995 and close to one million people being slaughtered, is a case in point. The most densely populated country in Africa, Rwanda had the world's highest fertility rate, according to the British medical journal the *Lancet*. Who's to blame? "The fact that any country should now be in intensely Catholic Rwanda's predicament is an indication of the world's and especially the Holy See's reluctance to face the issues of population control," says the *Lancet*.

Because of this reluctance, in many countries there isn't enough water or arable land to provide sustenance for all the people. In her 1992 book *Last Oasis: Facing Water Scarcity*,

Sandia Postel cites twenty-six countries with a combined population of some 230 million people suffering from water scarcity in the early 1990s. The shortage of water in the Middle East is illustrative. Speaking in the May 14, 1992, *Washington Post*, Elias Salameh, founder and director of the University of Jordan's Water Research and Study Center, made the following prediction:

> No matter what progress irrigated agriculture makes, Jordan's natural water at this pace will be exhausted in 2010. Jordan then will be totally dependent on rain water and will revert to desert. Its ruin will destabilize the entire region. . . . None of the regional countries—Egypt, Israel, Jordan, Syria, Saudi Arabia or the gulf emirates—can be self-sufficient in food in the foreseeable future, if ever. All Middle East economies must be restructured away from agriculture because of a lack of water.

Yet agriculture remains the predominant source of work in most developing countries. Michael Renner of the Worldwatch Institute says that, in Rwanda, "half of all farming took place on hillsides by the mid-eighties, when overcultivation and soil erosion led to falling yields and a steep decline in total grain production." Overcultivation can then lead to a work shortage. Out of a global workforce of more than two billion people, at least 120 million are unemployed and another 700 million are underemployed or without enough income to meet basic human needs.

Linking the problems, Renner notes that "the Hutu leaders that planned and carried out the genocide in 1994 relied strongly on heavily armed militias" who were recruited primarily from the unemployed. "These were the people who had insufficient land to establish and support a family of their own and little prospect of finding jobs outside agriculture," Renner continues. "Their lack of hope for the future and low self-esteem were channeled by the extremists into an orgy of violence against those who supposedly were to blame for these misfortunes."

The Vatican's Opposition to Birth Control and Abortion

The future with regard to overpopulation need not continue to be so dim. Although unbridled capitalism and the greed of corporations and their allies in politics bear responsibility for world poverty, unemployment, and the degradation of the soil, air, and water, the Vatican's success in organizing opposition on a worldwide level to any reduction of population is chiefly to blame.

The May 28, 1992, *New York Times* reports that "in preparation for next month's Earth Summit in Rio de Janeiro, Vatican diplomats have begun a campaign to try to insure that the gathering's conclusions on the issue of runaway population growth are not in conflict with Roman Catholic teaching on birth control." The pope has gone so far as to issue a decree to Catholics that states: "In the case of an unjust law such as a law permitting abortion . . . it is never lawful to obey it or to take part in a propaganda campaign in favor of such a law or vote for it."

Reprinted by permission of Ann Telnaes.

In the United States, the Vatican succeeded in getting enough support from right-wing Catholics and Protestants in Congress to block the United States from paying its debt to the United Nations by attaching an amendment to ban the use of federal funds by any private or government organization that supports abortion overseas or counsels women on where to get an abortion. These politicians are part of a coalition that has effectively captured the Republican Party, the House of Representatives, and much of the federal judiciary; it is within about two seats of changing the nature of the Supreme Court. Its influence has grown enormously in state legislatures, as well.

The Vatican, of course, wields tremendous power, but it doesn't speak for all Catholics. In the June 19, 1992, *National Catholic Reporter*, editor Tom Fox writes: "I feel the church is causing great harm to the planet, making millions suffer unnecessarily, and is compromising its teaching authority to boot, by its absolutist, narrowly defined birth control position."

Jennifer Mitchell, in the January/February 1998 *World Watch* magazine, writes:

> In the developing world, at least 120 million married women and a large but undefined number of unmarried women want more control over their pregnancies, but cannot get family planning services. This unmet demand will cause about one-third of the projected population growth in developing countries over the next fifty years, or an increase of about 1.2 billion people.

The Need for Safe, Legal Abortion and Effective Contraception

It is significant that the *Lancet* has said, "No country has achieved smaller families or low maternal mortality without access to safe abortion . . . and none will in the foreseeable future." The World Health Organization estimates that 585,000 women die each year during pregnancy and childbirth. However, according to the 1997 *Vital Signs*, "The death toll underestimates the magnitude of the problem. For every maternal death as many as 30 women sustain oftentimes crippling and lifelong health problems related to pregnancy." Moreover, many of these deaths and lifelong health problems could have been prevented by access to family planning services and safe, legal abortion.

It is also important to mention that more than 4.7 million people, most of them in southeast Asia and sub-Saharan Africa, contracted HIV in 1995 and 1.7 million people died from AIDS. The Vatican has also strongly opposed any funding of contraceptives such as condoms, which can help prevent sexually transmitted diseases.

What all this means is that the so-called pro-life movement is really a pro-death movement—and we must begin to call it that, not only because of the population wars but because it is denying reproductive freedom to women worldwide and rejecting prevention of disease. But we, too, deserve some of the blame. We are too silent, too inactive, too complacent, too compliant.

Legalized abortion and contraceptive birth control are not only essential for the reproductive freedom of women, they, along with maintaining strong public schools, are where the crucial struggle to maintain separation of church and state must continue to be waged. Now is the time—before it's too late—to make humanism real by organizing and acting, by working with others, to raise the consciousness of a nation and a world, to save a planet.

> "*In the face of overpopulation in the poorer countries, instead of forms of global intervention at the international level—serious family and social policies, programs of cultural development and of fair production and distribution of resources— anti-birth policies continue to be enacted.*"

Contraception and Abortion Are Unethical

John Paul II

In his encyclical letter entitled *Evangelium Vitae*, or "The Gospel of Life," Pope John Paul II of the Roman Catholic Church charges that many modern societies are sliding toward a "culture of death" that supports abortion and euthanasia. The pope argues that abortion is wrong because it is the destruction of life, and that contraception is unethical because it contradicts the idea that sex is an act of procreation. The pope believes that overpopulated nations should be given economic and social support rather than having abortion and contraception foisted upon them.

As you read, consider the following questions:

1. In what ways are abortion and contraception "specifically different evils," according to the pope?
2. What types of global intervention does the pope recommend as alternatives to promoting abortion and contraception?

Excerpted from *The Gospel of Life (Evangelium Vitae)* encyclical letter of Pope John Paul II, 1995.

Today there exists a great multitude of weak and defenseless human beings, unborn children in particular, whose fundamental right to life is being trampled upon. If, at the end of the [nineteenth] century, the Church could not be silent about the injustices of those times, still less can she be silent today, when the social injustices of the past, unfortunately not yet overcome, are being compounded in many regions of the world by still more grievous forms of injustice and oppression, even if these are being presented as elements of progress in view of a new world order. . . .

This reality is characterized by the emergence of a culture which denies solidarity and in many cases takes the form of a veritable "culture of death." This culture is actively fostered by powerful cultural, economic and political currents which encourage an idea of society excessively concerned with efficiency. Looking at the situation from this point of view, it is possible to speak in a certain sense of a *war of the powerful against the weak:* a life which would require greater acceptance, love and care is considered useless, or held to be an intolerable burden, and is therefore rejected in one way or another. A person who, because of illness, handicap or, more simply, just by existing, compromises the well-being or life-style of those who are more favored tends to be looked upon as an enemy to be resisted or eliminated. In this way a kind of *"conspiracy against life"* is unleashed. This conspiracy involves not only individuals in their personal, family or group relationships, but goes far beyond, to the point of damaging and distorting, at the international level, relations between peoples and states.

In order to facilitate the spread of *abortion*, enormous sums of money have been invested and continue to be invested in the production of pharmaceutical products which make it possible to kill the fetus in the mother's womb without recourse to medical assistance. On this point, scientific research itself seems to be almost exclusively preoccupied with developing products which are ever more simple and effective in suppressing life and which at the same time are capable of removing abortion from any kind of control or social responsibility.

It is frequently asserted that *contraception*, if made safe and available to all, is the most effective remedy against abortion. The Catholic Church is then accused of actually promoting abortion, because she obstinately continues to teach the moral unlawfulness of contraception. When looked at carefully, this objection is clearly unfounded. It may be that many people use contraception with a view to excluding the subsequent temptation of abortion. But the negative values inherent in the "contraceptive mentality"—which is very different from responsible parenthood, lived in respect for the full truth of the conjugal act—are such that they in fact strengthen this temptation when an unwanted life is conceived. Indeed, the pro-abortion culture is especially strong precisely where the Church's teaching on contraception is rejected. Certainly, from the moral point of view contraception and abortion are *specifically different* evils: the former contradicts the full truth of the sexual act as the proper expression of conjugal love, while the latter destroys the life of a human being; the former is opposed to the virtue of chastity in marriage, the latter is opposed to the virtue of justice and directly violates the divine commandment "You shall not kill."

But despite their differences of nature and moral gravity, contraception and abortion are often closely connected, as fruits of the same tree. It is true that in many cases contraception and even abortion are practiced under the pressure of real-life difficulties, which nonetheless can never exonerate from striving to observe God's law fully. Still, in very many other instances such practices are rooted in a hedonistic mentality unwilling to accept responsibility in matters of sexuality, and they imply a self-centered concept of freedom, which regards procreation as an obstacle to personal fulfillment. The life which could result from a sexual encounter thus becomes an enemy to be avoided at all costs, and abortion becomes the only possible decisive response to failed contraception.

The close connection which exists, in mentality, between the practice of contraception and that of abortion is becoming increasingly obvious. It is being demonstrated in an alarming way by the development of chemical products, intrauterine devices and vaccines which, distributed with the same ease as contraceptives, really act as abortifacients in the

Reprinted with permission from Chuck Asay and Creator's Syndicate.

very early stages of the development of the life of the new human being. . . .

Another present-day *phenomenon*, frequently used to justify threats and attacks against life, is the *demographic* question. This question arises in different ways in different parts of the world. In the rich and developed countries there is a disturbing decline or collapse of the birthrate. The poorer countries, on the other hand, generally have a high rate of population growth, difficult to sustain in the context of low economic and social development, and especially where there is extreme underdevelopment. In the face of overpopulation in the poorer countries, instead of forms of global intervention at the international level—serious family and social policies, programs of cultural development and of fair production and distribution of resources—anti-birth policies continue to be enacted.

Contraception, sterilization and abortion are certainly part of the reason why in some cases there is a sharp decline in the birthrate. It is not difficult to be tempted to use the

154

same methods and attacks against life also where there is a situation of "demographic explosion."

The Pharaoh of old, haunted by the presence and increase of the children of Israel, submitted them to every kind of oppression and ordered that every male child born of the Hebrew women was to be killed (cf. *Ex* 1:7–22). Today not a few of the powerful of the earth act in the same way. They too are haunted by the current demographic growth, and fear that the most prolific and poorest peoples represent a threat for the well-being and peace of their own countries. Consequently, rather than wishing to face and solve these serious problems with respect for the dignity of individuals and families and for every person's inviolable right to life, they prefer to promote and impose by whatever means a massive program of birth control. Even the economic help which they would be ready to give is unjustly made conditional on the acceptance of an anti-birth policy.

Humanity today offers us a truly alarming spectacle, if we consider not only how extensively attacks on life are spreading but also their unheard-of numerical proportion, and the fact that they receive widespread and powerful support from a broad consensus on the part of society, from widespread legal approval and the involvement of certain sectors of health-care personnel.

As I emphatically stated at Denver, on the occasion of the Eighth World Youth Day, "with time the threats against life have not grown weaker. They are taking on vast proportions. They are not only threats coming from the outside, from the forces of nature or the 'Cains' who kill the 'Abels'; no, they are *scientifically and systematically programmed threats*. The twentieth century will have been an era of massive attacks on life, an endless series of wars and a continual taking of innocent human life. False prophets and false teachers have had the greatest success." Aside from intentions, which can be varied and perhaps can seem convincing at times, especially if presented in the name of solidarity, we are in fact faced by an objective *"conspiracy against life,"* involving even international institutions, engaged in encouraging and carrying out actual campaigns to make contraception, sterilization and abortion widely available. Nor can it be denied that the mass media are often implicated in this conspiracy, by lending credit to that culture which presents recourse to contraception, sterilization, abortion and even euthanasia as a mark of progress and a victory of freedom, while depicting as enemies of freedom and progress those positions which are unreservedly pro-life.

| "*There is a wide, if not universal, consensus among governments of developing countries that their rate of population growth is too high.*"

Population Control Programs Benefit Developing Nations

Charles F. Westoff

In the following viewpoint, Charles F. Westoff, a professor of demographic studies and sociology at Princeton University, argues that the problem of rapid population growth in developing nations is serious enough to warrant government intervention. One means of reducing fertility rates in developing nations is to ensure women's reproductive freedom so that they are not pressured, by their culture or their husbands, into reproducing. However, Westoff cautions that, in contrast to the claims of women's advocates at a recent international conference on population, merely empowering women will not ensure a decline in fertility rates. An effective population control program, says Westoff, must also provide contraception to women and use television and radio to promote the desirability of small families.

As you read, consider the following questions:

1. What percentage of feminist groups' demands were incorporated into the Cairo report, according to Bella Abzug, as paraphrased by the author?
2. What is the total fertility rate for the African continent for the years 1990–1995, according to Westoff?
3. What four policy suggestions does the author present to further the effectiveness of population control programs?

Excerpted from "International Population Policy," by Charles F. Westoff, *Society*, May/June 1995. Reprinted with permission from Transaction Publishers. All rights reserved.

The 1994 International Conference on Population and Development is now history. Even before the delegates left Cairo there was a rush to proclaim the meeting a triumph. Despite the fact that the abortion controversy captured the daily headlines and all but paralyzed progress on other topics for most of the meeting, the U.S. delegation claimed a major victory in the consensus reached by the representatives of the 180 governments in attendance. Since so many have been so pleased with the outcome, a few reservations may be in order; but first a few observations on the magnitude of the problem.

The delegates in Cairo were confronted with a world population approaching 5.7 billion and growing at a rate that, if continued, would double that in little more than forty years. The increase of close to one billion people in the 1990s alone is the greatest increase in a decade in history, even though the rate of growth is declining. Vice President Al Gore, in his remarks at the opening of the conference, dramatized the time perspective of this growth:

> We would not be here if we did not think that the rapid and unsustainable growth of human population was an issue of the utmost urgency. It took 10,000 generations for the world's population to reach two billion people. Yet over the past fifty years, we have gone from two billion to more than five-and-a-half billion. And we are on a path to increase to nine or ten billion over the next fifty years. Ten thousand generations to reach two billion and then in one human lifetime—ours—we leap from two billion toward ten billion.

Population Control vs. "Reproductive Rights"

These are forceful words, nowhere to be found in the Cairo report. Perhaps it is the deadening language of international meetings or the pervasive sensitivity to national sovereignty that leads to platitudinous recommendations. Or perhaps it was the effect of the women's well-organized efforts to substitute their own agenda, which enshrined the "empowerment of women" and reproductive health concerns. Demographic targets were dismissed as potentially coercive. In a spirit of elevating the level of discourse, the population subject per se was submerged in the rhetoric of reproductive rights and "sustainable development." In fact, it became almost mandatory to explicitly denigrate the whole subject of population growth and subordinate it to other issues. This tendency was reflected succinctly in the remarks of Egypt's President Muhammad Mubarak, who was the host of the meeting:

> ... the population problem facing the world today cannot be correctly solved on the basis of handling the demographic dimensions only; it should be dealt with in close relation to the problems of social, economic and cultural development. Improving women's conditions, especially in developing countries, is the cornerstone of any demographic policy.

This reluctance to deal directly with the issue of high fertility and the tendency to bury the problem in other related subjects is dramatically evident from one calculation that an earlier draft produced an estimated 1,170 recommendations (a staggering number), of which only a dozen directly addressed population growth.

More than for either of the preceding international population conferences, women's issues have greatly influenced, if not dominated, the Cairo report. The organized feminist groups were extremely successful in this respect (Bella Abzug claimed that 70 percent of their demands were incorporated). The final document contains three chapters that reflect this influence: "Gender Equality, Equity, and Empowerment of Women," "Reproductive Rights and Reproductive Health," and a chapter on the family. The last topic had earlier provoked a major dispute, since "the family" was not seen by many as an appropriate model for a society in which various permutations of the traditional structure increasingly occur. One recurring important theme is the emphasis on female education, since that seems to be related to contraceptive behavior and fertility.

Empowering Women Is Not Enough

The problem with much of this report is not that any of the long list of recommendations is objectionable. Quite the contrary: they are collectively admirable even if utopian. The problem is that so many of these objectives—women's education or reproductive health or reproductive rights, for example—should be promoted in their own right rather than rationalized as instruments to reduce fertility. Nor is the last connection, between reproductive rights and reduced fertility, even made clear; indeed, the objective would seem to be to give women the right to be able to have the number of children that they want. The assumption, never clearly addressed, is that if this ideal materialized, fertility would decline significantly. In more general terms, the argument is that all that has to happen to resolve the population problem is to enable women to realize their own reproductive ends.

Feminist Opposition to Population Control

Many feminists ignore or minimize population growth and its presumed consequences, saying efforts to address the issue will inevitably lead to population control programs and fertility rate targets—in other words, to coercion of women by governments. (It's as if the consequences of rapid population growth apply only to men.) Some feminists argue that the emphasis on fertility control is misplaced: the real problems are gender inequality and poverty. Even family planning, long the centerpiece of women's efforts to gain control over reproduction, is not seen as an unambiguous benefit; radical feminists are suspicious of many birth control methods. . . .

It is curious that some organized feminist groups, in the name of reproductive rights, seem determined to dilute the population objectives of the United Nations conference. So much potential common ground exists in the goals of the family planning movement and in women's concerns for their reproductive health and rights—as well as for improving their status—that it would be perverse if extremist feminist groups managed to deflect a worldwide effort to address the population question head-on.

Charles F. Westoff, *New York Times*, February 6, 1994.

This rationale is not new. It was proposed originally more than twenty years ago against the recent history of the baby boom in the United States in the report of the Commission on Population Growth and the American Future, where, in fact, it was an appropriate policy. The prevention of unwanted births would have been more than sufficient to reduce the fertility rate in the United States to the replacement level. Enabling women to realize their reproductive preferences is a much more politically acceptable approach than aiming for zero population growth (the euphemism for "population stabilization" was also invented in the U.S. report). In the Third World today there are also countries in Latin America or Southeast Asia where the elimination of unwanted fertility would have a similar demographic effect. But in many developing regions—much of the Middle East and sub-Saharan Africa—such a policy would have little demographic impact. In sub-Saharan Africa, it would imply a total fertility rate (TFR) of five rather than six births per woman, which leaves a considerable distance to the two-birth average needed for replacement.

Rapid Population Growth Is Harmful

However muted in the Cairo report, there is a wide, if not universal, consensus among governments of developing countries that their rate of population growth is too high. Arguments about how damaging this growth is for the environment or for social and economic development will never be settled definitively. The reasonable assumption is that, at the very least, rapid population growth intensifies environmental and developmental problems and makes their solution more difficult. But the population "problem"—obviously more than just numbers, as the policy pundits repeatedly point out—can be seen dramatically in the numbers that current rates imply. The case of Africa is instructive.

The total fertility rate for the African continent in 1990–1995 is estimated to be just under six births per woman, with a 1990 population of 633 million persons. Let us assume that the fertility rate remains unchanged to the middle of the [twenty-first] century. By the year 2050—within the lifetime of many young people alive today—the population of Africa would reach nearly five billion, close to the number of people in the whole world today. The point of this projection is not that this is likely to happen—indeed, the Malthusian check of increasing mortality would undoubtedly be triggered. The point simply is to show how unsustainable such population growth would be. Add to this the negative rates of economic growth that currently exist through much of sub-Saharan Africa, and a truly nightmarish picture emerges. Such potential growth says two things: It makes the debates about the relationship between population growth, environmental degradation, and economic development seem academic, and it indicates that such high fertility rates simply cannot be sustained. . . .

Policy Responses

We begin with the premise that the high rate of population growth in the world, almost all of which is occurring in developing countries, is a matter of serious concern. It is true that the environmental impact of the product of population and per capita income is far greater in the developed than in the developing countries, but fertility in the North is low and environmental issues are best addressed by economic, political, and technological responses rather than by population policy. The main population problem is the high fertility in many developing countries—a proposition that seems to offend political sensibilities in the Cairo report. The high rates of population growth—2 to 3 percent per annum—are the consequence of rapid declines in mortality with a significant lag in the decline in fertility.

What, then, is the appropriate policy response? In my view, there are several paths that could and should be followed.

Provide Contraception and Create Incentives for Small Families

The unmet need for already existing family planning should be satisfied. One estimate, derived by others from my work on the subject, is that there are 120 million women who want to postpone the next birth or avoid further childbearing altogether. Satisfying this latent demand, however, involves much more than simply supplying contraceptives. Many such women say that they do not intend to use any method of contraception because they are ambivalent about further childbearing, or they are ignorant of contraception, or they are concerned about health implications or side effects of contraception, or they have religious objections, or their husbands would be opposed, and so on. So satisfying unmet need involves much more than providing contraceptive supplies; it involves educational and informational efforts as well. Nevertheless, it is obviously sensible to try to meet existing demand. In some parts of the world, for example, in Thailand, Sri Lanka, Colombia, or Brazil, if this unmet need were completely satisfied, it could lower fertility to replacement or below replacement. It would have some depressing effect on fertility everywhere except probably in China, where, if couples' preferences prevailed, fertility would probably rise.

Second, a demand for small families should be created. Since satisfying unmet need in certain parts of the world will fall far short of reducing fertility sufficiently, the demand will have to be developed. This is clearly more difficult than satisfying unmet need, in part because we are not sure which avenues to pursue. The conventional wisdom about promoting education, especially the education of women, although certainly desirable, would require secondary educational levels; it would be extremely expensive for many governments, and it would also require radical reorganization of household economies in many parts of the world. But increasing education is a worthwhile goal in itself, and efforts in this direction would be welcome and would probably have the byproduct of reducing fertility.

Since economic development is a universal goal, the demographic effects will probably be similar to those experienced historically in the West. How long all of this would take is a major question, but at least the aim of lowering fertility is compatible with the desired social and economic development goals.

Use Mass Media to Promote Family Planning

Another more immediate and more practical possibility lies in the use of the mass media to communicate the desirability of fertility control and small families. We know that there is a strong association in many developing countries between using contraception or preferring fewer children and exposure to radio, television, and the print media generally. Presumably, the effect lies in the exposure to Western or modern styles of life, the emphasis on individualistic values, consumer behavior, and so on. Experience with more focused efforts to use the media to promote family planning is also accumulating. The most interesting approach is the production of soap operas to communicate in dramatic form the advantages of postponing pregnancy and marriage, of the spacing of births, of fewer children, and of gender equality. Such soap operas have been broadcast in Kenya, India, Mexico, Brazil, the Philippines, and elsewhere. There is one about to begin in China aimed at extolling the advantages of the very small family and the importance of the girl child. Cross-sectional studies and other evidence have suggested a strong effect on contraceptive behavior and reproductive attitudes. There is now a national study in Tanzania with a classical experimental design to evaluate the effects of a radio soap opera aired two nights a week on a variety of measures of reproductive behavior. If the results of this experiment and the evaluation in China live up to expectations, the acceleration of such broadcasts may be considerable.

A third policy path is to encourage efforts to increase age at marriage. There are some obvious gains to be realized from delaying marriage and childbearing. As noted above, it can offset some of the growth resulting from the demographic momentum of the youthful age structure. In theory, it would also reduce the incidence of teenage childbearing. These effects assume that fertility will continue to occur largely within marriage and that the age of the mother at the first birth will be affected commensurately. There is evidence that both the mean age of women at first marriage and at first birth is increasing in many countries. How could such a trend be accelerated? Increasing the minimum legal age at marriage, which has been done in some countries, probably would have some limited effect. The increasing education of women seems to make an important contribution to later ages of marriage. The determinants of age at marriage are similar to those affecting family planning and fertility and are all embedded in the same constellation of social change. It is also an objective that can be included in mass media communications. It has been featured in the soap-opera approach. . . .

Governments Have a Role to Play

These policy responses would be greatly facilitated with the active support of central governments along with continuing international assistance. The attitude of the government and its willingness to take action is clearly relevant. The extreme case is China, which has a policy and a successful program that many regard as coercive. This may be partly the result of ignoring the problem for decades. Reducing the rate of population growth was for years deemed ideologically objectionable in China, inconsistent with Marxist doctrine. Eventually, the inconsistency was rationalized away as a need for population "planning," in the same sense that steel or agricultural production is planned in the socialist economy. In Kenya, which is experiencing a rapidly accelerating fertility decline, observers also credit the commitment of the government both in promoting and legitimizing concern about rapid growth, propagandizing for fertility control, and supporting family planning programs. Thailand, Bangladesh, and Indonesia are other examples of countries whose governments aggressively support policies to reduce fertility. On the other hand, other governments have expressed concern for decades but have not been very successful in curbing fertility—Pakistan is a case in point. Although fertility has declined in many states of India, the birth control policies were disastrous. As my late colleague Frank Notestein wisecracked with great prescience years ago: "The sterilization program of the Ghandi government seems more likely to bring down the government than the birth rate."

One of the obvious difficulties that governments have in promoting population policies is that other economic and political problems are more immediate and therefore more pressing. It takes a certain level of statesmanship to try to enact controversial policies and programs to improve the lot of the next generation.

Avoiding the Sensitive Issue of Population Control

The main problem with the latest international effort in Cairo to address the issue of future population growth is not in what was said but in what was avoided. Despite some rhetoric to the contrary by various world leaders in the beginning, the Cairo report lacks any sense of urgency about the large increase in numbers on the horizon. In promoting all of the good things in life, it manages to reduce the problem to individual rights. In Paul Demeny's words:

> I think that articulating population programs simply as yet
> another need-satisfying welfare program, without invoking
> the rationale that prompted these programs in the first
> place—government concerns about the harm caused by too-
> rapid aggregate population growth—greatly weakens the ar-
> gument that these programs should be a high priority.

One yearns for a simple declarative sentence in the Cairo document that says that high fertility in many developing countries is a major problem and that a demand for smaller families must be generated.

The good news from Cairo is the promise of a significant infusion of money into the field; however, a third of that is slated for women's reproductive health and HIV/AIDS-prevention programs. The conference was a resounding success for the advocates of women's reproductive health but a disappointment to many concerned about population growth. And the two are not synonymous.

"*[Developing nations] question the right of
rich countries, who are unwilling to change
their lifestyle of excessive consumption, to
demand changes in the lifestyle of poor
families.*"

Current Population Control
Programs Do Not Benefit
Developing Nations

Seamus Grimes

In the following viewpoint, Seamus Grimes argues that many
population control programs are ineffective and unethical.
These programs, says Grimes, which stress the importance
of providing birth control and abortions to women rather
than improving the economies of developing nations, have
been designed by the United States and other industrialized
nations in order to protect their own societies from an influx
of immigrants and the increased consumption of resources.
Seamus Grimes is a professor of geography at the National
University of Ireland.

As you read, consider the following questions:

1. What euphemisms have replaced the terms "birth
   control," population control," and "abortion" in
   discussions of population policy, according to Grimes?
2. In the 1960s, according to P.J. Donaldson, what simplistic
   solution did the U.S. government decide was the answer
   to population growth in Third World nations?

Excerpted from "From Population Control to 'Reproductive Rights': Ideological
Influences in Population Policy," by Seamus Grimes, *Third World Quarterly*, vol.
19, no. 3, 1998. Reprinted by permission of the author.

For many years the population debate has been framed within a very narrow perspective based on an economic orthodoxy which claimed that rapid population growth created a barrier to economic development, particularly in the least developed parts of the world. The widespread acceptance of this analysis gave rise to a consensus about how to deal with the problem, which involved providing access throughout the less developed world to contraception and other forms of fertility control. Increasingly, however, this orthodoxy and consensus is being questioned, and alternative forms of explanation are emerging which provide an impressive critique of what is now regarded as a simplistic analysis. . . .

As more attention is given to some of the influences which moulded the thinking behind the emergence of population control ideology, one of the factors which needs to be examined is the growing concern with the demographic marginalisation of the West, arising from differential fertility, or with high rates of population growth in the southern hemisphere occurring simultaneously with below-replacement level fertility throughout the industrial world. Neo-Malthusian thinking about the links between environment, population and resources has had considerable influence on policy formulation, particularly in the Third World context. Harvey points out that, once 'connotations of absolute limits come to surround the concept of resource, scarcity, and subsistence, then an absolute limit is set on population. And the political implications of terms such as overpopulation can be devastating.'

B. Duden traces the emergence of population as a major policy issue to the late 1970s, when the objective of controlling and managing population in policy statements took on images of an explosion of mainly yellow and brown people in countries that could not repay their debts. Once the *underdeveloped* were identified as outbreeding the North, and at the same time frustrating their own progress, controlling population became a newly defined goal. . . .

During the past three decades at least 35 million migrants from the South [the southern hemisphere, which consists mostly of developing nations] have taken up residence in the North, with around one million joining them each year. Another million or so are working overseas on contracts for fixed periods, while the number of illegal migrants is estimated to be around 15 to 30 million. In outlining what he calls a new 'global apartheid', A. Richmond refers to the efforts of the wealthy countries of North America, Europe and Australasia to protect their affluent lifestyles from the imminent threat of mass immigration from poor countries.

From the outset, language has played a fundamental role in framing the debate about population policy. Between the 1930s and the 1960s, before the US government became officially involved in promoting population control as a major foreign policy objective, terminology such as 'birth control' and 'population control' was in common usage. The thinking of the early generation of population control enthusiasts was strongly influenced by eugenics and racism, and they were much less subtle in stating their objectives publicly than more recent advocates. As the USA became more involved in population policy, however, there was an acute awareness of the need to camouflage direct government involvement by working through private population organisations. There was also an awareness of the need to modify and manipulate the use of language, in order to package population control policy for the Third World in terminology that was more politically acceptable. Thus 'birth control' became 'family planning', and 'population control' became 'population assistance'. The much more politically sensitive issue of abortion has given rise to euphemistic terminology such as 'menstrual regulation': more generally the discourse about fertility reduction is now conducted primarily within the feminist terminology of 'reproductive rights'.

Reliance on Outside Funding Has Biased Demographers

One of the most remarkable features of the most recent period of population studies in the USA is the growing number of studies putting forward an incisive and hard-hitting critique of the use of the science of demography to provide the intellectual justification for population control policy. While much of the critique focuses on American demography in recent decades, the influence of nineteenth and early-twentieth-century advocates of birth control and eugenics, such as Marie Stopes and Margaret Sanger, on demographic thinking should also be alluded to. Sanger, in particular, was alarmed over global population growth and she had considerable success in mobilising scholars in the 1920s, which led to the formation of the International Union for the Scientific Study of Population and the Population Association of America.

It should be noted that Paul Demeny, who was Vice-President of the Population Council in New York for a number of years and continues as editor of the Council's journal, *Population and Development Review*, has been a consistent critic for a long period of the narrow and isolationist view of population taken by both demographers and policy makers. In an area of study which did not welcome hostile criticism, his critique remained something of a lone voice within demography until more recently. Demeny identifies the heavy reliance on external funding as one of the main factors which posed a serious threat to the intellectual integrity of demography in recent decades. This forced demographers to accept criteria set by donors, which were not always consistent with standards of scholarship. He accuses demographers of being 'intellectually unprincipled' by putting service to policy makers above concern with intellectual integrity. . . .

Origins of US Population Policy

Despite the general perception that international policy on population issues has evolved primarily through the work of United Nations agencies, and in particular through the United Nations Population Fund (UNFPA), the role of the US government, in promoting population control should not be underestimated. A detailed analysis of the thinking behind US involvement in population policy between 1965 and 1980 has been carried out by P.J. Donaldson. Donaldson, who worked as part of the family planning establishment in both Thailand and South Korea, and who supports the goal of reducing Third World fertility levels, provides a reasonably objective and critical account of developments during this period.

Donaldson explains how a relatively small elite involved in the family planning movement succeeded in influencing public opinion to the extent that the US government officially joined the movement to slow Third World population growth in the mid-1960s. Based on a simplistic analysis of the problem, the focus of the solution was quite narrow, concluding that women in developing countries were producing too many children, and that they had to be provided with access to the means of birth control. There was little or no understanding of the social and economic circumstances of the people involved, and no real interest in researching the complexities of the situation.

Although there was an element of paternalistic humanitarianism motivating the movement to control rapid population growth, the thinking was schizophrenic from the outset, with a major influential factor being the determination to preserve US economic and political interests around the world. While there was a widespread consensus that rapid population growth would hinder economic development in poor countries, there was a greater concern with the potential threat to US interests which could arise from a rapidly expanding and unstable Third World. It was clear to politicians and policy analysts and to influential foundation officials that people in developing countries could not aspire to the equivalent of a US lifestyle.

The vision of the world which helped to define the US response to what was defined as 'the population crisis' was one dominated by the USA and its Western allies. There was a growing consciousness of demographic displacement of the developed world by a rapidly expanding Third World population. There was also an acute awareness of economic interdependence between the USA and the Third World, particularly in terms of the need to guarantee the supply of essential raw materials, minerals and oil. In 1980 the National Security Council identified the fact that the USA would be the desired destination of so many of the world's emigrants and refugees as a major policy issue for the USA.

An important US government document, the *National Security Study Memorandum 200 (NSSM 200)*, providing insight into the political rationale for population control in less developed countries, is ignored by Donaldson. *NSSM 200* resulted from a directive by President Nixon in 1974 to undertake a study to determine the 'Implications of World Population Growth for US Security and Overseas Interests'. The study was completed in the same year and became declassified at the end of 1980. With the realisation that there 'could be a serious backlash with some LDC [less developed country] leaders seeing developed country pressures for family planning as a form of economic or racial imperialism', it noted how vital it was 'that the effort to develop and strengthen a commitment on the part of the LDC leaders not be seen by them as an industrialised country policy to keep their strength down or reserve resources for use by the rich countries'. It stated bluntly that 'the goal was fertility reduction and not improvement in the lives of people', and referred to the need for the 'indoctrination of the rising generation of children regarding the desirability of smaller families'.

Population Control as Foreign Policy

During the late 1960s and early 1970s the movement to control fertility transformed itself from being the preoccupation of enthusiasts in family planning organisations to becoming official US state policy in relation to the developing world. Donaldson outlines the growing links between the State Department, the U.S. Agency for International Development (USAID), the Population Council, the Ford Foundation, the International Planned Parenthood Federation (IPPF), the Peace Corps and population studies centres in a number of universities, including Johns Hopkins, Columbia, Michigan, North Carolina and California. Funding for international population policy activities steadily increased from the 1960s, but there was considerable effort to protect US interests by camouflaging the extent of government involvement in overseas population programmes. USAID was advised to 'keep out of sight, out of print and out of politics in Latin America', where there was strong resentment of US interference, and to channel aid through IPPF, the Pathfinder Fund and other such organisations.

While IPPF and its network of affiliates around the world played an important role, the UNFPA was the key agency involved in gaining legitimacy for this extremely sensitive policy, and the World Bank also became one of the major sources of funding for population activities. The US government played a key role in ensuring the establishment of the UNFPA, and was responsible for most of its funding through USAID during its early years, ensuring that it had considerable control over its activities. In the period since then, the relationship between the US government and the UNFPA has varied according to the policy of particular administrations.

While the role of the USA in influencing population control policy continues to be significant, other developed countries, particularly Scandinavia, the UK and Germany, have also played an important role in funding population programmes. The most significant source of funding for such programmes in recent years has been Japan, which announced in 1994 that it would commit US$3 billion over the period from 1994 to 2000 to combat global population problems. It is ironic that a country in which both the contraceptive pill and sterilisation were illegal until recently should display such enthusiasm for the extension of access to fertility control in the less developed world.

Population Programmes Must Do More

In addition to convincing the political establishment that rapid population growth was a serious threat to the interests of the developed world, the population community also argued in favour of supplying the Third World with all forms of birth control devices together with access to sterilisation and abortion. In the run-up to the most recent UN population conference in Cairo, which had as one of its chief objectives an increase in funding for population activities to around $17 billion a year by the year 2000, a senior economist in the World Bank, L.H. Pritchett, published a paper in the *Population and Development Review* arguing that the contraceptive approach towards solving fertility control had been a failure. . . .

Pritchett argues that, rather than increasing the supply of contraception or other forms of fertility control to women in poor countries, fertility reduction is best seen in the context of improving economic and social conditions. . . .

In their desire to justify increased expenditure on population programmes, the population community has inferred a causal link between contraceptive access and variations in fertility. Pritchett suggests that what he is arguing is well known among the experts who have been promoting contraception for many decades, namely that the fundamental change that needs to take place is a desire for lower fertility, and that this will involve more than the relatively cheap solution of subsidising contraceptive services. . . .

The US Pressures Third World Nations to Accept Fertility Control

The debate on population policy issues [has not taken] into account the view of people living in poor countries towards fertility control. At the international level, A. Najam has traced the evolving perspective of developing countries towards population policy, as displayed in particular by their involvement in the three UN conferences on population at Bucharest, Mexico City and Cairo. He suggests that, while these countries are not necessarily opposed to population control, and many of them have introduced quite vigorous fertility control programmes, they have consistently rejected interference and intervention from the industrialised North because of their concern with their own sovereignty. They see no incompatibility between pursuing population programmes domestically, and rejecting any suggestion of treating population issues as an international question. They insist that the best approach towards dealing with population problems is to promote development, alleviate poverty and create the conditions of security in developing countries whereby poor people would not feel the need to have large families.

Despite the rhetoric of these international conferences, however, the general view within the South is that the only transfer of resources they are likely to see coming from the rich North will be related to population activities. There is considerable suspicion within the South towards this emphasis on population issues among the richer countries of the North, and there is a strong resentment of the growing tendency to regard population growth in the South as a major source of environmental degradation. They question the right of rich countries, who are unwilling to change their lifestyle of excessive consumption, to demand changes in the lifestyle of poor families in the South in relation to their pattern of procreation. With the USA reverting to its pro–population control agenda at the Cairo conference, Najam claims that a major concern of the South is that funds will be diverted from development assistance and into population programmes. A further reason for this fear is the declining geopolitical significance of the South in the post–cold war period, and the growing trend to divert aid to the Eastern European economies in transition. . . .

Coercive Fertility Control Programmes and Civil Rights

The management and implementation of fertility control programmes fall within the jurisdiction of the governments of developing countries and, in cases where non-democratic regimes are in power, these programmes have frequently resulted in a disregard for and abuse of the human rights of the target populations. C.A. McIntosh and J.L. Finkle refer to the recent rise of an ethical critique arising from the significant body of evidence of such abuse in many countries. The best known cases have been the coercive one-child policy in China and the programme of mass sterilisation in India, but there has been considerable evidence of coercion in many other countries. In the case of China, S. Geenhalgh and J. Li suggest that 'birth planning programmes' rather than the more euphemistic 'family planning programmes' would describe such operations more accurately. It is notable that many of the researchers, who have felt it necessary to highlight the ethical issues involved, are clearly not opposed to the overall objective of limiting fertility levels in developing countries.

The dilemma raised by this critique is centred on the conflict between the rights of individuals in relation to procreation and societal goals which are determined by governments. Warwick wonders 'how much procreative freedom can be tolerated' before it affects the security of a nation or a community. While many developing countries have introduced population policies in recent years, frequently under duress from World Bank loan conditionalities and from consistent pressure from other organisations such as USAID, such policies link the extent of procreative freedom within these countries with the self-interest and security concerns of the developed world. . . . While the tolerance of a certain degree of procreative freedom is being determined by their own governments, the range of options of many of these governments is in turn being severely restricted by international forces.

Population Control Programs Are Racist

We should stop funding [United Nations Population Fund] programs which, in effect, tell people in Africa, Asia, and Latin America that we want fewer of them. The U.S. and other developed nations must be partners in economic development, not neocolonial masters. Our aid programs should respect human dignity, not denigrate the worth of human beings. The massive, monomaniacal bias toward population control in our current "aid" programs is unjust, discriminatory and frankly racist.

Population Research Institute, *Money for Nothing: Why the United States Should Not Resume UNFPA Funding*, 1999.

Despite the Cairo rhetoric of 'reproductive rights', the ethical critique reveals many cases where political expediency has resulted in the suppression of civil liberties. Warwick suggests that, by their silence, donors [to population control programs] have become tacit supporters of coercion and pressure being used against poor populations. . . . In the early stages of promoting fertility control in developing countries, some programmes undoubtedly violated many ethical principles in seeking ways to overcome the tremendous resistance which they encountered. More recently, some sections of the international feminist movement have highlighted the oppression of women and the neglect of their health arising from the implementation of fertility control programmes. One of the most serious criticisms relates to programmes with demographic targets, which subject women's needs to impersonal societal goals.

Much of the concern of studies dealing with the ethics of population policies is related to threats to the free choice, welfare, justice, and even physical survival of women targeted by fertility control programmes. Financial incentives and disincentives limit freedom and violate justice, particularly when they are used against the poorest and least powerful members of society. Such incentives are sometimes restricted to sterilisation and intra-uterine devices (IUDs), which can result in medical complications for a significant proportion of acceptors. The mortality rate from IUDs in the Third World is roughly double what it is in the West, because of infections and sceptic abortions. Free choice is also limited by the refusal to remove IUDs, or hormonal implants such as Norplant, which prevents pregnancy for five years or more, despite the serious side effects which such devices can inflict on women. . . .

Clever Repackaging of the Same Agenda

Within the feminist movement there are clear divisions between those who regarded the 1994 Cairo Conference as a step forward in the promotion of a more liberal approach towards the provision of 'reproductive rights', and those who regard the politically correct language of reproductive choice, women's empowerment and environmental concern as a clever repackaging of the population establishment's old agenda of fertility control. The World Bank, which increased its funding for population activities to £2.5 billion in 1995, and which offers 100% funding only to projects which promote some aspect of fertility reduction, was the main focus of attack of some feminists at the time of the Cairo conference. Vandans and Shiva, for example, claimed that 'the World Bank has cleverly redefined the "population and development" sector as "population and women" thus making invisible the destructive impact of its policies on the lives of Third World women and ironically appearing as a champion of women's rights.

Referring to the Cairo conference, a recent editorial in the *Lancet* (22 July 1995) criticised the 'new colonialism of the international women's health agenda' as a dangerous strategy, because it placed 'western utopianism before local pragmatism'. It was particularly critical of the attempt to define health narrowly in terms of fertility control. This results in a situation throughout many parts of the developing world where the emphasis is on coercing women to adopt fertility control, while neglecting the provision of primary health care. It has also been argued that, since the UNFPA is no longer sure about its justification for seeking to limit population growth, its programme of action for Cairo suggests the new solution of exporting the West's sexual revolution to the developing world. Since the Western lifestyle, characterised by the centrality of the individual, has already brought about a downward spiral in fertility levels in developed countries, population planners are now convinced that introducing major changes in cultural, social and religious values will bring about a similar result in the less developed world. Between 1986 and 1990 the Johns Hopkins University Population Communication service received in excess of $100 million in funding from USAID to develop radio and television series for the promotion of family planning services in sub-Saharan Africa.

Current Policies Are Misguided and Unethical

A review of the literature taking a critical look at the influences underlying population control policy reveals a number of disquieting aspects about how this policy has taken shape, based on a rather simplistic analysis of the issues involved. Much of the literature reviewed in this [viewpoint] focuses on the key role of the USA in influencing the political backing and funding for controlling Third World fertility. While some evidence reveals a rather paternalistic and philanthropic humanitarianism influencing the policy environment on these issues, it is clear that the domestic concerns of developed countries, and particularly the USA, played a major role. Such concerns included fears about political stability, guaranteeing the supply of essential resources, and the possibility of being invaded by large numbers of immigrants and refugees from less developed countries. . . .

The tendency to impose population policies based on rational scientific interpretations has also resulted in the widespread abuse of human rights in the implementation of fertility control programmes. The intensifying ethical critique of such programmes emerging from various sources, including some sectors of the international feminist movement, questions the meaningless rhetoric of reproductive choice used in documents of large institutions such as the World Bank as they impose coercive policies on poor countries, resulting in higher infant mortality and lower levels of schooling. Such policies have been shown to be counterproductive because they are derived from ethnocentric thinking whose objective is to transform the backwardness of target populations. The unfortunate possibility is that much of the powerful critique of policies to date will be ignored by a population establishment which is motivated by factors other than the welfare of families in poor countries.

"If the right to have children isn't worth defending, even to the point of death, then what is?"

Coercive Population Control Programs Violate Human Rights

Steven W. Mosher

In the following viewpoint, social scientist Steven W. Mosher describes China's population control policy, in which each family is permitted to have only one child. After the first child is born, says Mosher, women are forced onto birth control; abortions are forced on couples who attempt to have a second child; and parents with two children are involuntarily sterilized. The author contends that China's population control program is a gross violation of privacy and reproductive freedom. He believes that the one-child policy, and the way it is enforced, is reason enough for the Chinese people to rebel against their communist government. Steven W. Mosher is president of the Population Research Institute in Front Royal, Virginia, and has written several books about China, including *A Mother's Ordeal: One Woman's Fight Against China's One-Child Policy.*

As you read, consider the following questions:
1. How does Mosher describe what he calls China's latest "'family planning' weapon"?
2. What international organizations does Mosher say support China's one-child policy?
3. According to the author, what is the purpose of the 1985 Kemp-Kasten Amendment?

Excerpted from "Are the Chinese Ready for Liberty and Self-Government?" by Steven W. Mosher, *The American Enterprise*, July/August 1998. Reprinted with permission from *The American Enterprise*, a national magazine of politics, business, and culture.

It has been 18 years since the most draconian population control program of modern times was imposed on Chinese families by their own government. In a 1979 speech, Deng Xiaoping drew the first outlines ("Use whatever means you must to control China's population. Just do it"). By 1981 the one-child-per-family limit was ironclad nationwide.

Mandatory Birth Control

The "technical policy on family planning"—a kind of how-to manual for Chinese officials—followed two years later. Still in force today, this *mandates* birth control for women of childbearing age with one child, sterilization for couples with two children (usually performed on the woman), and abortions for women pregnant without permission. Abortions are performed throughout the entire nine months of pregnancy, even up to the point of childbirth. It is common to give lethal injections to viable infants *in utero* or, if their mothers are brought in to the hospital already in labor, as they begin their descent into the birth canal. I once interviewed the head of a large military hospital in South China who admitted to me that in his facility alone some 400 cases of infanticide (he delicately referred to them as "procedures") were committed each year.

In the mid-'80s, according to Chinese government statistics, birth control surgeries—abortions, sterilizations, and IUD insertions—were running at a rate of 30 million a year. Numbers for more recent years are unavailable; the government, embarrassed by reports of coercion and female infanticide, has refused to release them. Many—if not most—of these operations are performed on women whose "consent" has been wrung from them by an escalating series of threats and punishments. "You will be fired from your job unless you comply" is a common form of arm-twisting.

Forced Abortion and Sterilization

China's population control officials have been known to abort and sterilize women by force, a fact which comes through sometimes in odd ways. In October 1997, for instance, Beijing proudly unveiled its latest "family planning" weapon: A mobile abortion unit. The occasion was the 24th

International Population Conference, hosted by Beijing and attended by 1,400 delegates from around the world. A white van rolled up to the conference hall as official Zhou Zhengxiang explained to the delegates China's plans to make 600 of these units to travel around the countryside. The rear door was thrown open for inspection and the delegates were invited to inspect its equipment. They saw a bed, suction pumps, and—a body clamp. *A body clamp.*

Quite apart from the cruel way it is enforced, the one-child policy constitutes an incredible expansion of raw state power. The Chinese Communist party has, in effect, intruded itself into the bedrooms of every couple in China, expropriated their reproductive tracts, and is dictating to them the number and spacing of their children. As far as reproduction is concerned, China's command economy is alive and well.

Over the years, I have given hundreds of talks on China's one-child policy, describing how it runs roughshod over the rights of women and families. With the exception of a few population control zealots, I have found that most Americans, when they learn the details, react strongly against what the Chinese government is doing. At the conclusion of my talk someone almost invariably raises the question: "Have there been protests against the policy?" Sometimes the point is put more bluntly: "Why don't the Chinese rebel?"

Pervasive Fear of the Regime

But the Chinese people have not rebelled against the one-child policy. There has been no organized resistance, and local demonstrations have been few. Violence has been limited to occasional acts of revenge against family planning officials by distraught husbands and fathers. The vast majority of Chinese have chosen the path of quiet accommodation rather than confrontation.

Why? One reason is pervasive fear of the regime. China's government so cows most of its people that they attend closely to the state's desires and behave accordingly. The Chinese government has a well-deserved reputation for harsh treatment of dissidents of all kinds. Few countries exact a higher price for protesting government policy.

This is especially true in the area of birth control. The birth control regulations of Guangdong Province contain, within a section called "rewards and punishments," a chilling warning to those who oppose the provincial government's will: "Those who attempt to defeat the birth control plan by engaging in rumor-mongering, distorting the truth, attacking and harming birth-control workers and activists, and generally breaking the law must be dealt with severely. If they have actually obstructed the implementation of the birth control plan, then they must be brought before the law for punishment. Those enemies of the people who attempt to defeat the birth control plan must be exposed immediately and resolutely attacked."

Opposition to the one-child policy, in other words, is treason, and such traitors—counterrevolutionaries in Communist parlance—are severely punished. Thus, citizens who are conscientiously opposed to the program dare not make any public expression of disapproval. One doctor told me that many of his colleagues were very upset about having to abort women who were seven-, eight-, and nine-months pregnant, but that no one had considered protesting publicly or refusing to perform such operations. "The consequences would be very serious," he told me. "There would be criticism, transfer, demotion, struggle, perhaps even hard labor. No doctor I know is prepared to take that risk."

The Silent Peasants

The peasants, whose security, privacy, and families are most threatened by this program, are for the most part politically inarticulate and naive about matters beyond their own rice bowl. The largest demonstration of which I am aware came in Jiangxi province in 1982, when peasants from six counties marched on a prefectural capital in opposition to the one-child policy. Occasionally, protest has gone beyond the merely vocal and become violent as well, as happened in a village in the Pearl River delta when a local official took a woman seven-months pregnant by force to the local abortion clinic. Her husband went into a black fury and killed the official's two sons, then committed suicide himself.

Aside from those who are directly affected, however, there

are not many who risk confrontation with the authorities over the birth control law's profound human rights abuses. The worst excesses of the campaign are occurring in the countryside, while China's few dissidents are concentrated in the cities, where their attention is held by other issues. Moral outrage is limited as well by the sometimes "nasty, brutish, and short" character of life in China, and by the lack of a religious tradition grounded in the sanctity of human life. Man is not made in God's image in the Chinese mind. And Confucius never said, "Thou shalt not kill."

A Right Worth Defending

Still, the timidity of the response seems out of proportion with the severity of the offense. One would think that if the Chinese people were ever going to stand against the tyranny of their government they would do so as a result of its taking their children away from them. If the right to have children isn't worth defending, even to the point of death, then what is?

It's impossible to imagine such a policy being successfully imposed on Americans. If the Clinton administration tomorrow announced a one-child policy (I assume Vice-President Gore, who apparently believes that babies cause global warming, would do the honors), the resulting reaction would bring down the government. Millions of Americans would literally grab their guns and head for the hills over such a policy. So why don't the Chinese rebel?

It is not as if the Chinese have never turned against their rulers. Faced in the past with rapacious officials or onerous taxes, there would be angry talk in local teahouses. In the wake of foreign mishaps or domestic calamity, whispers would spread that the emperor had lost the Mandate of Heaven—the God-given right to govern. Dispossessed or starving peasants sometimes became roving bandits, attacking isolated government garrisons or granaries. From time to time over the long course of Chinese history—every half-century or so—widespread armed rebellion would break out. Every two or three centuries, when conditions grew particularly intolerable, it would be successful.

But since 1979, living standards have been on the rise—

rapidly in most parts of China—and so the restrictions on childbearing have been balanced by economic bounty. The Chinese people have accepted that trade-off. The Chinese Mandate of Heaven, it would seem, has more to do with putting food on the table than with putting babies in the cradle.

The Preference for Male Children in Many Developing Nations

The one-child policy has created a situation where there are very few females in the entire nation. A girl conceived in China has to run an eerie kind of gauntlet if she is to survive. The first threat she faces is sex-selective abortion because many parents will use the ultrasound technique at about 20 weeks and, if it reveals that the baby is a girl, they'll abort her. If it reveals the baby is a boy, they'll celebrate. They're only allowed one child and they prefer a boy.

The second part of the gauntlet comes at birth. Many couples who don't have access to the ultrasound technology decide beforehand that if their newborn baby is a girl, she is not going to be allowed to live. So at birth, they either suffocate her, plunge her into a bucket of water and drown her, or abandon her by the side of the road to die of exposure.

Some of the little girls who are abandoned end up in state-run orphanages that are really killing fields. Babies in this circumstance die within a few days or a few weeks. Basically, China's state-run orphanages are part of the enforcement mechanism of the one-child policy.

The next part of the gauntlet is that even older little girls are sacrificed if their mother becomes pregnant with a son. A family will give up a little two-year-old or three-year-old girl because if they didn't, they would have to abort a newly conceived child that might be, or is known to be, a boy. And they want a son who will support them in their old age.

Steven Mosher, *New American*, 1999.

Post-Mao China has seen protests, of course, the most famous being those that occurred in Tiananmen Square from April 18 to June 4, 1989. But these were led by unmarried students as yet unaffected by the strictures on childbearing. Other issues, from democratization to dormitory housing, dominated their agenda. And the brutal way these demon-

strations were put down underlined once again the willingness of the regime to use deadly force against its oppo-
nents—and made even more unlikely any mass protests
against the one-child policy.

The United Nations Supports China's Policy

Another factor blunting popular discontent is widespread international support for the one-child policy. Organizations
such as the United Nations Population Fund (UNFPA) and
the International Planned Parenthood Federation have been
encouraging the anti-population campaign of the Chinese
government from the beginning. Generous funding has been
forthcoming, along with awards and laurels, and the Beijing
regime has trumpeted this, telling its people the whole world
approves of what it is doing. How it must dampen the spirit
of population dissidents to learn that, however noxious the
government's policies, the United Nations approves.

So successful has China's domestic propaganda campaign
been that student leaders who escaped to the U.S. following
the Tiananmen massacre were surprised to learn their government's one-child policy was controversial in this country.
They had been told that the U.S. government and people
supported the birth restrictions. The truth, of course, was
quite the opposite. Far from applauding the one-child policy,
most elite opinion in the U.S. has condemned it. The U.S.
Congress in 1985 actually forbade any U.S. funds from going
to a country (read: China) or organization (read: UNFPA)
that supported forced abortion or sterilization. The Kemp-
Kasten Amendment was signed into law by President Reagan.

The Government They Deserve?

It is often said that a people get the government they deserve. Does the apparent willingness of the Chinese people
to tolerate brutal assaults on their family life reflect some
deep passivity in the national character? Do they suffer from
some culturally ingrained fatalism that makes them easy prey
for despots who happen along? Is it possible they are, to put
it bluntly, culturally unfit for democracy?

Out of the reach of Communist authorities, younger Chinese have been bold enough. Following Tiananmen, for ex-

ample, overseas Chinese organized some 8,000 groups in opposition to the Beijing regime, and a number included the one-child policy on their lists of human rights grievances. Many of these groups, especially those composed of students from the PRC [Population Research Center], were eager to learn more about democracy.

From 1989 to 1993, as director of the Asian Studies Center at the Claremont Institute, I and other Institute personnel organized a dozen or more symposia for Chinese pro-democracy leaders. We were eager to help educate them in the principles of liberty and the mechanics of democracy. We taught them Robert's Rules of Order, so that they could debate political issues in an atmosphere free of fear. We translated the U.S. Constitution into Chinese, to make it more accessible to the Chinese people. We encouraged discussion on the principles of self-government. In these efforts we were, to judge from the positive responses of the symposia participants, largely successful.

But at the same time, we realized that democratic structures wouldn't survive long in China unless they could rest securely on a Chinese historical and cultural foundation. So we went back to the works of Confucius, Mencius, the Legalists, and others, hoping to find references, however oblique, to such concepts as popular sovereignty, separation of powers, and the like.

In this effort we were by and large disappointed. There is no Chinese tradition of respect for human rights, indeed, no notion of inalienable rights at all. There is no ghost of a suggestion that government in any way derives its just powers from the consent of the governed. From the beginning of Chinese recorded history, the emperor has been an absolute despot. In this regard, there is little to distinguish Qin Shihuang, who ruled from 221–206 B.C., and Mao Zedong, who ruled from A.D. 1949–1975. China's autocratic traditions provide no roots, and precious little foothold, for the foreign shoots of democracy.

Possibilities for Democracy in China

This is not to say that China's democratization is impossible, merely that it will be difficult. For in fact, some of the beginnings of Chinese democratization have already been laid. The Republic of China, founded on the mainland in 1911, was self-consciously modeled upon the United States, with its separation of powers and a presidential, rather than parliamentary, political system. This was destroyed when the Japanese invaded and the Chinese Communist party came to power.

Yet, out of reach of the People's Liberation Army, the Chinese on Taiwan have continued the progression. While the mainland was in the grip of a totalitarian regime run by the megalomaniac Mao, Taiwan in the 1950s and '60s was busily gaining experience in local democracy, by holding election after election at the county and township level. And over the past two decades, as the People's Republic practiced its peculiar brand of Leninist capitalism, Taiwan has successfully made the transition from autocratic state to modern democracy. The Chinese people, the example of Taiwan demonstrates, are capable of self-government.

We should not expect democracy to come as quickly to China as it did to Taiwan, however. Cultural and political change were greatly accelerated in Taiwan, a small, island nation cut off from the mass of China and utterly dependent on the United States. Within such a context, the U.S. example of ordered liberty and respect for human rights quickly carried the day, overwhelming within a generation the traditional notions of autocratic rule. Changing the political culture of China will take longer. Much longer.

> "*If exercise of [the right to have children] is leading to universal disaster, is it not time that the possibility of modifying it was at least considered?*"

Coercive Population Control Programs Are Necessary

John B. Hall

John B. Hall argues in the following viewpoint that because of the terrible effects of overpopulation, people should sacrifice their freedom to reproduce and governments should institute mandatory fertility control programs. However, Hall does not support China's fertility reduction program, in which the government interferes directly in people's reproductive decisions. Instead, Hall, a professor of microbiology at the University of Hawaii, suggests the possibility of creating a contraceptive vaccine and then engineering a virus that could carry this form of contraceptive throughout the globe, thus reducing fertility levels worldwide.

As you read, consider the following questions:

1. According to Hall, people have become numb to the enormous amount of human suffering in the world and have ceased to respond to the pain of others. What problems has this led to, in the author's opinion?
2. What reasons does the author give for his belief that a reduction in worldwide population is unlikely to come about voluntarily?
3. What analogy does Hall use to describe the moral dilemma presented by the possibility of releasing his theoretical infectious contraceptive virus?

Excerpted from "Negative Population Growth: Why We Must, and How We Could, Achieve It," by John B. Hall, *Population and Environment*, September 1996. Reprinted with permission from the author and Plenum Publishing Corporation.

Humanity has been all too successful in remodeling much of the natural world to serve its own purposes. While this has permitted an unprecedented increase in the number of humans that the Earth will support, it appears that we have exceeded the limits of our natural life-support systems and are rapidly destroying the very resources needed to sustain our existence. We need to turn to the conquest of one last frontier, perhaps the most difficult and dangerous one of all, the mastery of ourselves.

A prosperous, healthy, educated, humane, and democratic form of life for everyone would require the numbers of people consuming the world's resources to come into some sort of reasonable balance with those resources. A brief look at the list of pressing world problems will make it obvious that the present world population is already far greater than can be sustained, even at present levels of misery, for very many more generations.

The Negative Impact of Humans on the Earth

Modern economic systems have an absolute dependence on massive utilization of fossil fuels which are being consumed at an extravagant rate, and which, of course, are not being renewed. Severe problems exist in finding adequate replacements for the enormous amounts of energy represented by this rapidly diminishing resource. Meanwhile, the carbon dioxide being produced threatens to alter the climate of the Earth via the greenhouse effect, with possible dramatic rises in sea level, bleaching and destruction of coral reefs, and the inundation of heavily populated, and often agriculturally vital, coastal areas. Soil erosion is removing topsoil 20 to 40 times as rapidly as it is being replenished at the same time that burgeoning populations require more and more food, and dwindling forests are cleared to provide the necessary extra crop land. Attempts to farm or graze marginal lands has led to rapid desertification of vast areas. Pollutants in the atmosphere destroy ozone and allow increasing fluxes of ultraviolet light to reach the Earth's surface, not only leading to increases in human skin cancer, but potentially damaging crop plants and reducing agricultural productivity. Many arid areas are irrigated by pumping ground water to the surface, often at rates far in excess of natural recharge—another short-sighted mining of a limited resource that cannot continue for long. Most fisheries are in trouble, with many in a state of near collapse as increasing efforts lead to less and less return, and only a total ban on fishing for a few years will allow recovery of some stocks. Rain forests and old growth forests at all latitudes are rapidly being cleared in the presence of an accelerating demand for wood products. Replanting and natural regrowth lag far behind this destruction, another example of the human propensity to consume resource capital even though the income that could have been derived from it will be needed in the future. Such drastic modifications of the natural environment are accompanied by the extinction of innumerable species, which are vanishing far more rapidly than they can be described and studied.

Growing Numbers of Poor

All of this has had enormous impact on human societies. Famine, war, ethnic strife, and disease are prevalent. Urban ghettoes all over the world teem with people who cannot find useful employment. And as our sympathies are overwhelmed by the sheer mass of human suffering, we turn away from it in despair and cease to respond to the pain of others. Our range of concern narrows and narrows, until only those of our own race, culture, class, and religious group command our sympathies, and we hide behind the gates of closed, guarded communities or the boundaries of tribe or ethnic group and reject all others. This loss of civility impoverishes the spirit and we become indifferent to genocide, starvation, poverty, ignorance, and want, and willing to fight all others for the land, space, and resources needed for the maintenance and expansion of our own group. Death squads proliferate to murder those who are politically active or just inconvenient, and wholesale massacres of "alien" peoples become almost a matter of routine.

All of these things are related to the density of human populations and competition for the resources required for their welfare. With the present world population, many critical resources are being rapidly exhausted, and conflicts between peoples intensify even as unpredictable changes in climate and other factors affecting the livability of the Earth occur.

If we value human culture, treasure civility, democracy, education, health, and a high standard of living in general, there is evident need for not only an end to further growth of the Earth's population, but also an actual and substantial decrease in the number of people the Earth is asked to support.

Voluntary Fertility Reduction Is Unlikely

Many people are highly concerned about the population problem. International conferences are held, efforts are made to persuade world leaders of the seriousness of the problem, educational programs are launched, and family planning services are promoted. The rate of growth of the world population has slowed, and if present trends continue, the population should stabilize after "only" one or two more doublings. This will, no doubt, postpone disaster so that it arrives a few years later than it will if *no* decrease in growth rate had occurred, but will hardly prevent it.

The necessary decrease in population size is most unlikely to come about voluntarily. Those few countries where the birthrate is slightly below replacement level have generally become quite concerned and some have attempted to raise it again. No nation or cultural group likes to believe that it is dwindling in size. No country wants to feel that it is losing population and that its own people might soon be replaced by fecund foreigners who are clearly all too ready to move into its relatively "empty" spaces. Some countries are moving to defend borders. A decrease in world population will be peaceful only if it affects everyone, and not just the few highly advanced countries where it is found at present.

Reproductive Freedom Is Not a Right

Rapid reduction in population size is necessary to prevent disaster, but many cultures still value high fertility levels; generations may be required to change these attitudes. These generations we do not have. Most people in the population studies field assume that individual control over reproductive decisions is a basic human right, which can not be tampered with. Yet if exercise of this right is leading to universal disaster, is it not time that the possibility of modifying it was

China's One-Child Population Control Program Is Necessary

Family planning in China is pursued in complete accordance with the relevant principles and human rights requirements designated by the international community. China's family planning policies and programmes combine citizens' rights and duties, joining the interests of the individual with those of society. These conform to the basic principles outlined at the various international population conferences and have been established on the basis of the relationship of interpersonal interests under socialism. Never in any country are rights and duties absolute, but rather, they are relative. There are no duties apart from rights, or rights apart from duties. When there is conflict between social needs and individual interests, a means has to be sought to mediate it. This is something that the government of every sovereign country is doing. As China has a large population, the Chinese government has to limit the number of births of its citizens. This is a duty incumbent on each citizen as it serves the purpose of making the whole society and whole nation prosperous, and it is not proceeding from the private interest of some individuals. This is wholly justifiable and entirely consistent with the moral concepts of Chinese society. To talk about citizens' rights and duties out of reality in an abstract and absolute way does not hold water either in China or in any other country. In a heavily populated developing country like China, if the reproductive freedom of couples and individuals [is] unduly emphasized at the expense of their responsibilities to their families, children and societal interests in matters of child bearing, indiscriminate reproduction and unlimited population growth will inevitably ensue. The interests of the majority of the people, including those of newborn infants, will be seriously harmed.

Chinese Information Office of the State Council, "Family Planning in China," August 1995.

at least considered? When the consequences of any course of action are clearly highly destructive of human welfare, how can one maintain that, never-the-less, people have an innate right to pursue that course of action? I believe that we must not hinder the efforts of governments to restrict reproductive rights among their own people, in order to bring the human population of the Earth and of their country into balance with the long-term carrying capacity at the level of well-being that the population wishes to maintain.

It may be argued that the government machinery necessary to monitor the reproductive decisions of individual families and the constant interference with these decisions that would be necessary to maintain a sub-replacement level of fertility can not be afforded by most countries, would be inconsistent with a democratic system of government, and if attempted, would be the source of constant resentment and resistance. Only in highly authoritarian countries like China is an approach to this level of social control feasible, and even in China there appears to be widespread evasion of the rules in many rural areas. This would certainly be a cogent argument if a reduction of average fertility on a global scale required the imposition of government regulations and monitoring. However, there are alternative ways of achieving this objective.

A Contraceptive Vaccine

The immune system, which usually functions to protect us from disease, but also is involved in allergies and the rejection of transplanted organs, can be harnessed to contraception. A contraceptive vaccine has been suggested for veterinary use. In this application, the female animal to be sterilized is injected with preparations of the zona pellucida (the outer envelope of the egg cell) from a different species of animal. The injected female responds to this foreign material by producing antibodies against it. These antibodies, however, also recognize the different but related material on her own eggs, a process called "cross-reaction," and attack these, destroying them. The death of these egg cells in the ovary releases the controls on maturation of immature egg cells and they begin to develop. As they approach maturity, they are also recognized by the immune system and destroyed in turn. A run-away cycle of maturation and destruction follows, and within a few months all of the potential egg cells in the animal's ovary have matured and been destroyed, and the female has been nonsurgically sterilized. Such a dramatic procedure would probably have little application in human contraception except in rare cases in which the person concerned wished to be sterilized, and since it would probably induce menopause, is unlikely to be acceptable even then. However, many less absolute contraceptive actions can also be mediated by the immune system.

Many cases of natural infertility occur because the woman produces antibodies against sperm which are recognized as foreign bodies by her tissues. Vaccines could probably be developed that would stimulate more women to produce such antibodies with a corresponding decrease in their fertility. In yet another approach, women have been vaccinated with peptide sequences similar to those found in certain hormones involved in reproduction. Very effective vaccines can be produced by splicing gene segments for the desired peptide sequences into some of the genes of the vaccinia virus and then using this virus to vaccinate the subject, just as it was used to vaccinate against smallpox. The peptide sequences produced by the virus stimulate antibody formation, the antibodies would cross-react with the naturally occurring hormone in the woman's body, and reproduction could be inhibited. Many such alternatives that harness the immune system in the service of contraception are available.

Infectious Contraception

None of these approaches would represent anything other than an addition to the existing armory of contraceptive systems, except for one thing: vaccinia virus is used as a vehicle for stimulating the immune system because it grows locally in the body, and produces an effective stimulus to the immune system, but very rarely spreads spontaneously to other people. However, there is no reason why the required antigens (the substances that stimulate the immune system) could not be introduced into any other virus, such as one of the more than 200 viruses responsible for the common cold, that would spread spontaneously through the population, and thus could serve as a form of *infectious contraceptive*. Depending on the nature of the antigen used, and their response to it, infected individuals would have more or less reduced fertility levels for longer or shorter periods of time. The effects would necessarily be uneven and it is unlikely that all individuals or populations would be equally affected. If a variety of antigens and viruses were used, however, these differences would average out and the average global fertility could be reduced to any desired level. The technology to carry out this global fertility regulation is not visionary. All of the knowledge and techniques that would be required are available today. Probably the creation and release of a number of different agents would be necessary to reach the desired level of negative population growth, as the effect of any one would be likely to be partial and geographically uneven due to the random accidents of distribution and infection.

Obviously, the use of infectious contraceptive agents raises profound moral and ethical questions, especially that of informed consent and particularly if one assumes that choices about reproduction are intrinsically the sole right of the couples (or often the male partner?) concerned. However, it is quite plain that eventually the growth of human populations will be curbed, and almost certain that negative growth will occur, as population overshoots even the short-range capacity of the Earth to support it, and massive mortality from disease, famine, and genocide takes its course.

The World Cannot Afford Free Choice in Reproductive Decisions

We are in the position of a skilled hunter, perched on a mountain ridge, who sees a bus load of children stalled on a curve on an adjacent ridge, while a truck comes hurtling down the road above, oblivious to the hazard out of sight around the curve below. The hunter has no way of communicating with either party, but he could shoot the truck driver, or blow out a tire, with the almost certain result that the truck will leave the road on the next curve and plunge into the canyon, killing the driver but sparing the bus and its occupants. This is obviously a morally equivocal situation, yet to do nothing, though sparing the hunter any legal responsibility for the death of the trucker, is a morally questionable choice also, since the trucker as well as the children will almost certainly be killed in the collision. Similarly, failing to arrest and reverse the present growth of human populations will almost certainly lead to a devastating collapse in human numbers—the deaths of hundreds of millions or billions of people is quite likely. In the process many major ecosystems will be degraded beyond recovery, innumerable other species will become extinct and many irreplaceable non-living, nonrenewable resources will be exhausted. This will certainly impair the capacity of the Earth to ever again support human societies at a high level of culture and prosperity for any significant number of people, while at the same time insuring that the right to reproduce as one sees fit becomes meaningless as people lose the means to insure their own survival, much less to provide for the children they would like to bear. The trucker will die, whether the hunter shoots him or not. It is Hobson's choice, but we must accept the fact that free choice in reproductive decisions is the one freedom we cannot, in fact, afford, if we are to preserve any of the others.

*"The problem is not population; it is poverty.
We can reach zero-growth population, if
we expand the world economy fourfold and
share the proceeds equitably."*

Industrialized Nations Should Help Developing Nations to Modernize

Gerard Piel

Gerard Piel is the former editor of *Scientific American* and the author of *Only One World: Ours to Make and Keep.* In the following viewpoint, he argues that the next doubling of the human population, from 5 billion to 10 billion, can be the last—if richer, industrialized nations begin working now to help modernize poorer, developing nations. Once nations undergo the industrialization process and enjoy more stable economies, he says, the incentives to have many children dissipate. Fertility rates in the nations of North America and Western Europe, he says, have rapidly declined since the industrial revolution, and now it is imperative that this economic transformation be extended to the rest of the world.

As you read, consider the following questions:

1. What does Piel believe is the "most urgent challenge civilization now faces"?
2. What are the two phases of the "demographic transition" that accompany industrialization, as described by the author?
3. According to Piel, how much investment does Agenda 21 ask of developing nations, as compared with industrialized nations?

Excerpted from "Worldwide Development or Population Explosion: Our Choice," by Gerard Piel, *Challenge*, July/August 1995. Reprinted with permission from M.E. Sharpe, Inc., Publisher, Armonk, NY 10504.

No entry on the U.S. political agenda has fewer advocates than does "foreign aid." What little of it that remains in the budget carries forward subsidies to Cold War client states which are now relegated to holding the line against Muslim fundamentalism. The poor countries of the world had their last serious mention in U.S. policy in 1961, when John F. Kennedy made his only appearance at the U.N. General Assembly. There, he proposed that the industrial nations make the 1960s the "Decade of Development," and he pledged 1.0 percent of this country's gross national product (GNP) to the effort. Nothing came of that speech. Nothing like it has come from any president since.

But there was a time when U.S. citizens were in favor of giving economic and technical assistance to the poorer countries. That was at the end of World War II. For a few years, as they recoiled from the horror of that war, people all around the world embraced their sense of people as global family. Freedom from want had been declared an aim of the war by the Allies. They had spelled it out in the United Nations Declaration of 1942. In the "underdeveloped countries," which were then emerging from the disbanding colonial empires of the European industrial powers, people were to be lifted out of poverty. With grants and soft loans under the Marshall Plan, U.S. taxpayers financed the economic recovery of the mother countries of those empires—allies (excepting only the USSR) and former enemies alike. In Point Four of his inaugural address to an approving electorate in 1949, Harry S Truman proposed making the Marshall Plan global.

In its interim headquarters at Lake Success, the United Nations began considering what it would take to develop the underdeveloped countries. The estimate was the work of a "Group of Experts"—respected economists from both the industrial and preindustrial worlds. Two of the Experts—Theodore W. Schultz of the University of Chicago and W. Arthur Lewis of the University of Manchester—would share the Nobel prize in Economics in 1979. In effect, they reported, it was time to get on with the industrial revolution.

In the undeveloped nations, people were still living with the technology that begat the agricultural revolution 10,000 years earlier. Given the extant population growth (1.5 percent per annum), it would be possible (and advisable) to move 1.0 percent of the population each year into nonagricultural employment. With a net increase of 1.0 percent in per capita income from industry, and another 2.0 percent increase from improved (by industrial inputs) agricultural yield, incomes could be made to improve at twice the rate of population growth.

At $2,500 for each new industrial job, the Experts estimated the total capital requirement for this enterprise in development at $19 billion per year. Some of that requirement would be filled by domestic savings within the preindustrial countries themselves. Much the greater part of it would have to come from the industrial countries. The profit and interest-bearing part of that external investment would depend, however, upon antecedent investment. It would amount to $3 billion per year, and would be spent on the building of social capital and physical infrastructure. That kind of investment is customarily financed by taxes. That $3 billion would cost the industrial countries 0.5 percent of their combined gross domestic product (GDP), and would be generated by outright grants from their governments—a classic example of priming the investment pump. Foreign aid at that level would see the underdeveloped countries through their industrialization to self-sustained economic development by the year 2000.

Business leadership in Europe and the United States was ready to entertain this proposition. The Experts' estimate was only round one, of course. But it was of the same dimension as the ongoing, successful undertaking of the Marshall Plan. The Great Depression was still fresh in their memories. The postwar generation of business managers was receptive to imaginative ideas for countercyclical outlays by the government. But the dispatch of troops to Korea in June 1950 extinguished the vision of an organized campaign of economic development. Foreign aid never reached the 0.5 percent goal—much less the Kennedy 1.0 percent.

A Global Marshall Plan

Now, in 1995, the time has come to bring the vision of a global Marshall Plan into focus again. Getting on with the industrial revolution is the most urgent challenge civilization now faces. If foreign aid was being considered an act of common humanity at mid-century, it is now dictated by the exigencies of common survival. The population of the world has more than doubled since 1950—from 2.5 billion to 5.3 billion. The number of people living in direst poverty has increased to 1.3 billion—close to the total population of the underdeveloped countries in 1950. The population is doubling now again. The number in direst poverty could equal the present world population. A doubling after that would bring the human species close to full occupation of the Earth.

In order to stabilize the world's population at some sustainable level, the industrial revolution must be carried out worldwide. Natural population increase has ceased in the 20 percent of the world population that is represented by the industrialized countries. Fertility is approaching the zero-growth rate in another 20 percent of the population currently living in the pre-industrial countries. That is happening in countries that have gotten on with their industrial revolutions since 1950. The population explosion that distresses so many well-off people in the industrialized countries is confined to the countries where the revolution has lagged and is now arrested. The sooner the industrial revolution reaches people everywhere, the smaller will be the world's population. . . .

The Issue Is Poverty

The problem is not population; it is poverty. We can reach zero-growth population, if we expand the world economy fourfold and share the proceeds equitably. That would bring the poorest 20 percent out of poverty. The industrialized countries must climb out of their economic torpor and restart their economic engines. Outlays for foreign aid could help to provide the necessary stimulus. In most industrialized countries (especially in the United States), governments appear to be unwilling or unable to take the initiative.

The rich industrial country is an entirely new historical phenomenon. It is rich in the sense that none of its inhabitants need submit to toil and want. Poverty persists in the industrialized countries as a social institution. In the poor countries, rampant poverty is a familiar story. It exists as if by definition. Simply, there is not enough to go around. Even today, village people in the poor countries live very much as their forebears did when the agricultural revolution settled them in villages 10,000 years ago. They survive by the sweat of their brows. The biological energy of their bodies gets the means of subsistence to renew that energy, but not much more. With traditional tools and practice, they can increase the means of that subsistence only by bringing new land under cultivation.

Over the ten millennia of agricultural civilization, population increase proceeded at a near-zero rate. It doubled only seven times—from an estimated 5 million to 500 million around 1600. Malthus's principle of population approximately describes the equilibrium with the misery that bespoke the human condition. High birth rates offset high death rates. Through good times and bad, life expectancy hovered near twenty-five years of age. In most times and places, people could anticipate no improvement in their circumstances in the course of their lifetimes. A person could improve his circumstances only at the expense of others. Status and force served this purpose and built high civilizations on the output of the traditional technology of the agricultural revolution.

Industrial Revolution

Now, the industrial revolution has brought rich countries abruptly into history. In Europe, around 1600 (where and when the industrial revolution had its earliest beginnings), life expectancy was no greater than twenty-five years of age. With the increase of production running ahead of population growth, death rates fell and life expectancies lengthened. The high birth rates that had barely offset the formerly high death rates began to deliver net additions to the population. In the 18th century, the curve of population increased steeply. Henry Adams dated his "acceleration of history" from that period. He found he could measure it because "it took the form of utilizing heat as force, through the steam engine, and this addition of power was measurable in the coal output." By the end of the 18th century, the growth of the European population had exploded. It doubled its 50-million census (extant in 1600) four times and over to nearly 1 billion by the middle of the 20th century. It constituted one-tenth of the world population in 1600, but it grew to a full one-third of it by 1950, having avalanched on to all the other continents.

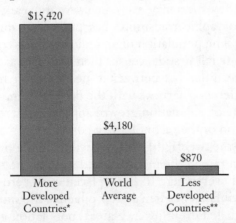

Per Capita Income in the Developed vs. the Developing World

*All of Europe and North America, Australia, Japan, New Zealand, and the republics of the former USSR.
**All countries not included in the more developed category.

Source: James A. Glynn, Charles F. Hohm, and Elbert W. Stewart, *Global Social Problems*. New York: HarperCollins, 1996.

During the 19th century, birth rates began to decline in the populations which were participating in the industrial revolution. At the outset, the birth control movement in Britain, on the continent, and in America found militant supporters. They recoiled from the other existing modes of population control—infanticide, abandonment, and abortion. The foundling hospitals and baby farms were evidence of their widespread practice. Too often, these institutions had fewer alumni than matriculates. During the first half of the 20th century, declining birth rates began converging with the declining death rates in all the industrialized countries. The European population explosion was coming to an end.

The Demographic Transition

By the middle of [the twentieth] century, demographers were recognizing an entirely new principle governing population growth— namely, that industrial revolution brings on a demographic revolution. In retrospect, it can now be seen that the population of the industrial world has made a transition since 1600 from near-zero growth at high death rates and high birth rates and life expectancy of less than thirty years to near-zero growth again at low birth rates and low death rates and life expectancy exceeding seventy years. Typically, this "demographic transition" has proceeded through two phases: (1) The population of an industrializing country sees its death rate fall first; its census then increases at rates measured by the difference between its death and birth rates; and (2) that difference narrows with the decline in the birth rate, and the rate of population growth approaches zero again.

Perfection of the technology of contraception around the middle of [the twentieth] century facilitated the final decline of the birth rate in the industrialized world. The total fertility rate fell everywhere to the replacement—zero-growth—rate of 2.1 infants per female reproductive lifetime. In some countries, it fell even lower. Natural population growth has all but ceased in the industrialized 20 percent of the world population. Immigration has brought most of its increase in numbers since 1950. . . .

The lengthening of life expectancy supplies the essential condition for restraint of fertility. People who can look forward to the full biologically permitted human lifetime permit themselves to be future dwellers. Assured of survival of their first infant(s), they can plan their families. Making the inverse Malthusian calculation, they see that the fewer, the more—for each. The family in industrial civilization (and in any zero-growth population) is necessarily a small family. . . .

The First Human Population

The population of industrial civilization can be said to be the first human population. The populations of other species offer up their young in great number to the pruning process of natural selection. Survivors die away from the youngest in the largest number at each stage of development or metamorphosis—down to the minority that survives to reproduce the species. Closer to nature, such was the age-structure of populations in agricultural civilization. It persists in the populations of the developing countries today. Industrial civilization brings very nearly all its newborn to full human growth and capacity. The youngest may be the smallest age group. Variation in the size of age groups up to the mortal eldest reflects differences, not in survival, but in decisions taken as to child-bearing in the parental age groups ahead. As mortality continues to yield to longevity, the eldest become the most rapidly growing age group.

The Benign Explosion

The population explosion that is rolling over the poor countries of the world may yet be recognized as a benign event. It declares the entrance of the rest of the human family into the first phase of the demographic transition.

Population growth began to rise above the near-zero rate in those countries early in their subjugation to the colonial empires of the European industrial powers. During the second half of the twentieth century, as the leading edge of industrial revolution crossed the borders of these former colonies, their population growth entered the explosive phase. The modest flows of foreign aid that emanated from the United Nations were sufficient to carry out the most portable technologies of industrial revolution. Most potent were those delivered by multilateral funding through the U.N. technical agencies. The World Health Organization brought the rudiments of preventive medicine and sanitation. The Food and Agriculture Organization brought seed and scientific practice. The Educational, Scientific, and Cultural Organization brought mass literacy campaigns. These inputs, domestic economic growth, and bilateral foreign aid from those industrial countries most interested in the country's market and resources induced a surge of development in all of the now-developing countries during the first two decades after World War II and into the 1970s. Consequently, life expectancy had lengthened by a decade on all the continents by 1990. As birth rates fell away from death rates, population-growth rates reached more than 2 percent in almost all the countries and more than 3 percent in some of them. "Explosion" is the appropriate word for this development. Comparable declines in the death rates of the existing industrialized countries transpired over the course of a century or two. . . .

From 1950 to 1970, the world's population-growth rate climbed to just over 2 percent. This was its all-time peak. The growth rate has been in decline ever since. That turning point declares the entrance of those developing countries which are proceeding most successfully with their development into the second phase of the demographic transition. The decline in their fertility rate (and now in their birth rates) is overtaking the decline in their death rates. When industrialization has brought the rest of the developing countries into the second phase, the world population-growth rate will go below 1.0 percent again, and will be headed toward zero.

Birth Rates Decline

For the present, this historic turning point is obscured from public understanding by its arithmetic. The declining growth rate is multiplying a larger population each year. Growth proceeds, accordingly, by the largest annual increments ever—in excess of 90 million people per year. If the decline in growth rate continues on its present slope, the annual increments will begin to shrink at the turn of the twenty-first century. That depends, of course, on the rate of development—especially in the poorest countries.

The neo-Malthusian alarm bells continue to ring. The cry is that "those people overpopulate their countries." In fact, the countries that have the highest population density—the seats of ancient civilizations in Asia—have moved most decisively into the industrial revolution and through the demographic transition. Africa, with the poorest and fastest-growing population, holds relatively the largest frontier open to human habitation.

In Latin America, disparity in income and wealth closes off another vast frontier to cultivation—the vast stretches of unused and underutilized latifundia. Meanwhile, the resources of these continents continue to fuel the economies of the industrial world. The underdeveloped countries await delivery of the less portable technologies of industrial revolution. Some day, these will permit them to develop the value of their resources for their own uses.

Neo-Colonial Economies

The sanctimony and controversy that have surrounded foreign aid have grossly inflated its dimensions in the public understanding. Except in the national budgets of the Nordic countries and Canada, outright grants for development have rarely exceeded 0.3 percent of the output of the industrialized world. For more than a decade, that which is properly reckoned a foreign aid in the U.S. federal budget has never exceeded 0.2 percent of the country's GDP. The percentage was higher when foreign aid served Cold War ends. Most of the flow then went to a half-dozen countries in East and Southeast Asia and to those at the eastern end of the Mediterranean. In South Korea and Taiwan, the fallout from aid and the huge military expenditure was big enough to trigger genuine development. That and the regional boom that occurred as a result of the Korean and Vietnam wars metamorphosed those countries—along with the city states of Hong Kong and Singapore. They became the celebrated "Tigers" of East Asia.

As early as the 1960s, private direct investment from the industrialized countries in plantations, mines, and oil fields began to overtake governmental outlays to foreign aid. The underdeveloped countries became the developing countries. What development most of them have seen (with the notable exceptions of India and China) is due principally to private investment. The contribution to development was indirect. Private investment (and the bilateral foreign aid it often entrained) went primarily to expedite delivery of the country's agricultural commodities, metal ores and, especially, petroleum to the dockside.

This engagement in world commerce has divided many developing countries (especially the smaller ones) into dual economies. The "modern" sectors operate in closer cultural, as well as economic, identity with the industrial powers most interested in their resources than with the traditional sectors in their own hinterlands. These countries remain in colonial status as "hewers of wood and drawers of water." They serve as sources of the raw materials most required by the industrialized world and, above all, of the petroleum that sustains industrial civilization in Europe and North America. In many countries, domestic political leadership (in half of them, military dictatorship) is content with this state of affairs. . . .

Renewing Foreign Aid to Developing Nations

As the U.S. media failed to report, Agenda 21 is the principal work product of the U.N. Conference on Environment and Development that convened in Rio de Janeiro in June 1992. Agenda 21 spells out and prices out the program of "sustainable development" that will sustain the fourfold multiplication of the global GDP that will be required in the [twenty-first] century to eliminate poverty in a world population that has doubled to 10-to-12 billion. It is a program of development the Earth can sustain in bringing the human species through its demographic transition.

Agenda 21 is composed of 2,500 enterprises engineered and otherwise realized by indigenous experts in the developing countries and U.N. technical agencies. They specify work to be done in environmental repair and conservation, in resource (especially agricultural resource) development, in the building of urban infrastructure, and in the development of human capital. The 2,500 enterprises constitute, of course, no more than a start on the work that must engage hundreds of millions of men and women in every developing country over the next century.

Agenda 21 shows that the task is finite and within the bounds of the Earth's resources. The developing countries are to supply most of the approximately $600-billion annual investment. From "savings" which are latent in their underemployed work forces and underutilized resources, they are committed to invest $500 billion—about 10 percent of their GDP. The industrial countries are asked to invest $125 billion—0.7 percent of their combined GDP. It will be transferred principally in the form of the technology necessary to catalyze the yield from people and resources. While the industrial countries signed the nonbinding document setting forth Agenda 21, they made no commitment to supply their 0.7 percent share. . . .

Agenda 21 asks, first of all, that the industrialized countries restart their economies. The electorates of those countries must soon assert their interest in the choice now being made by default. In the United States, apparently, the choice is to be deliberate. The "Contract with America" schedules the last best hope of Earth for zeroing-out to oblivion. For the survival of market economies and self-governing polities, the present doubling of the world's population must be the last.

Periodical Bibliography

The following articles have been selected to supplement the diverse views presented in this chapter. Addresses are provided for periodicals not indexed in the *Readers' Guide to Periodical Literature*, the *Alternative Press Index*, the *Social Sciences Index*, or the *Index to Legal Periodicals and Books*.

Diana Brown — "The Misery Behind the Statistics," *Free Inquiry*, Spring 1999.

Sonia Correa and Rosalind Petchesky — "Exposing the Numbers Game," *Ms. Magazine*, September 1994.

Nicholas Eberstadt — "Demographic Clouds in China's Horizon," *American Enterprise*, July/August 1998.

Nicholas Eberstadt — "What Is Population Policy?" *Society*, May/June 1995.

Laurie Garrett — "The Virus at the End of the World," *Esquire*, March 1999.

Mary Ann Glendon — "What Happened at Beijing," *First Things*, January 1996.

Cynthia Gorney — "Caught in the Crossfire: Will the War on Reproductive Rights Ever End?" *Utne Reader*, May/June 1998.

Susan Greenhalgh and Jiali Li — "Engendering Reproductive Policy and Practice in Peasant China for a Feminist Demography of Reproduction," *Signs*, Spring 1995.

Frances Kissling — "The Case Against the Vatican," *Free Inquiry*, Spring 1999.

Susan V. Lawrence and Emily MacFarquhar — "Drawing Battle Lines in Beijing," *U.S. News & World Report*, September 11, 1995.

Frances Mitsuka — "Islam and Birth Control: Not a Moral Conflict," *Middle East*, June 1993. Available from I.C. Publications, Box 261, Carlton House, 69 Gt. Queen St., London WC2B 5BN.

Peng Pei-Yun — "China's Population Policy," *Population and Development Review*, December 1997.

Nafis Sadik — "Human Rights: Women Have Special Needs," *Populi*, March/April 1998.

Carl Wahren — "Avoiding Future Shock," *Free Inquiry*, Spring 1999.

Charles F. Westoff — "What's the World's Priority Task? Finally, Control Population (Population Control and Feminism)," *New York Times*, February 6, 1994.

For Further Discussion

Chapter 1

1. Thomas Malthus did not consider contraception a viable "preventive" way to reduce fertility and thus control population. (His religious beliefs precluded this, and he wrote before many modern methods of contraception had been invented.) Discuss the importance of this omission.

2. Frederick Engels said that it is a "fact" that "children are like trees, returning abundantly the expenditure laid out on them." Do you think this is the case in modern, industrialized countries? Explain your answer.

3. John H. Fremlin saw the advance of science resulting in improved food production. Do you believe there are inevitable limits to increasing food production? If so, what are they?

Chapter 2

1. Together, the two viewpoints by J. Kenneth Smail and Max Singer constitute a broad prediction of population growth in the twenty-first century: Population will continue to rise dramatically until around 2050, at which time the number of humans on earth will begin to decrease sharply. The viewpoint by Barbara Crossette emphasizes that population decline will be most severe in richer, industrialized nations. Assuming that both these predictions are valid, which trend—the increase or decrease—do you feel is cause for more alarm, and why?

2. William B. Schwartz warns that medical advances that prolong life are a double-edged sword, since they could lead to overpopulation. He suggests that government policy makers direct medical research funding toward work that increases quality of life rather than its length. Do you agree with this proposal, or do you believe that the conquest of fatal diseases such as cancer should be a high priority?

Chapter 3

1. In their viewpoint, Lester R. Brown and his associates at the Worldwatch Institute list eleven ways in which overpopulation will harm the environment and decrease overall quality of life. How does Timothy W. Maier respond to such warnings? Do you feel that Brown and his colleagues may be exaggerating the dangers of overpopulation? Based on the evidence provided in each of the viewpoints, whose argument is more convincing, and why?

2. Both Don Hinrichsen and Nicholas Hildyard believe that world hunger is a serious problem. However, they each emphasize different ways of dealing with the problem. Describe in your own words each of the two authors' approaches to fighting hunger, and explain which one you think would be most effective.

Chapter 4

1. Consider the viewpoints by John M. Swomley and Pope John Paul II. Do their views on how the population debate influences the abortion controversy affect your own personal views about abortion? If so, how?

2. What role do you think the United States should play in population control? Do you agree with Charles Westoff that the United States is helping developing nations by supporting population control programs, or do you feel that Seamus Grimes is correct in his view that current population control programs may be unethical? How might Gerard Piel respond to Westoff's and Hall's views about population control?

3. Given the discussion of population control in this chapter, do you think that the right to have children is a basic human right? Explain why you feel it is ethical or unethical for governments to (1) pay for free education and child care to encourage population growth, (2) pay for free access to contraception, family planning education, and abortion in order to discourage population growth, and (3) limit by law the number of children a family may have. Finally, what is your view of John B. Hall's suggestion that scientists should engineer an "infertility virus" that makes one-third of the world's population infertile? In your opinion, what, if anything, makes some population control policies more acceptable than others?

Organizations to Contact

The editors have compiled the following list of organizations concerned with the issues debated in this book. The descriptions are derived from the materials provided by the organizations. All have publications or information available for interested readers. The list was compiled on the date of the present volume; names, addresses, and phone numbers may change. Be aware that many organizations take several weeks or longer to respond to inquiries, so allow as much time as possible.

Human Life International (HLI)
4 Family Life Lane, Front Royal, VA 22630
(540) 635-7884 • fax: (540) 635-7363
website: http://www.hli.org

HLI is a pro-life religious organization that opposes international population control efforts. It rejects the idea that overpopulation is a problem, and instead supports education, coupled with more humane governmental and economic policies, as the best solution to world hunger and environmental damage. Its monthly newsletter, *HLI Reports*, contains many articles on population control.

International Women's Health Coalition (IWHC)
24 E. 21st St., New York, NY 10010
(212) 979-8500
website: http://www.iwhc.org

IWHC supports women's reproductive health in the developing world via innovative health care programs and policy research. It offers educational materials on reproductive health and copublished the "Rio Statement" to represent a feminist position at the 1994 UN Conference on Population and Development held in Cairo, Egypt.

Negative Population Growth (NPG)
1717 Massachusetts Ave. NW, Suite 101, Washington, DC 20036
(202) 667-8950
website: http://www.npg.org

NPG is concerned with population and environmental issues and works to promote a decrease in U.S. and world populations. It publishes a triannual newsletter, *Human Survival*, and various position papers, including *Zero Net Migration*, *Beyond Family Planning*, and *Family Responsibility*.

Population Action International (PAI)
1120 19th St., Suite 550, Washington, DC 20036
(202) 659-1833
website: http://www.populationaction.org

PAI concentrates on policies and programs which would slow down the world's population by stressing the education of women and the voluntary use of contraceptives. It publishes fact sheets on new contraceptive devices and gives annual "Picks and Pans" awards to ten countries with the best and worst population programs.

The Population Council
One Dag Hammarskjold Plaza, New York, NY 10017
(212) 644-1300
website: http://www.popcouncil.org

The council conducts research on social science, biomedicine, and public health in order to improve the well-being and reproductive health of people living in developing nations. Its numerous publications include the quarterly *Population Development Review*, the bimonthly *Studies in Family Planning*, and books such as *Resources, Environment, and Population* and *The New Politics of Population*.

The Population Institute
107 Second St. NE, Washington, DC 20002
(202) 544-3300
website: http://www.populationinstitute.org

The Population Institute is an international organization concerned with the consequences of rapid population growth. It works to build awareness about overpopulation and advocates for measures to help stabilize population. It publishes the bimonthly newsletter *Popline* and the yearly report *World Population Overview*.

Population Reference Bureau
1875 Connecticut Ave. NW, Suite 520, Washington, DC 20009
(202) 483-1100
website: http://www.prb.org/prb

The Population Reference Bureau serves as a source for population statistics in the United States and the world. It publishes current data, identifies trends, and makes projections. The bureau publishes the quarterly *Population Bulletin*, the monthly *Population Today*, and U.S. and world population data sheets.

Population Research Institute (PRI)
PO Box 1559, Front Royal, VA 22630
(540) 622-5240
e-mail: pri@pop.org • website: http://www.pop.org

The Population Research Institute is a nonprofit educational organization that opposes population control programs that do not respect the dignity and rights of the individuals and the families. PRI works to document abuses of human rights in the name of population control, and to promote the material and social benefits of moderate population growth. It publishes the newsletter *PRI Review* and special publications such as *Know Your Rights!* and *The Facts of Global Depopulation.*

United Nations Population Fund (UNFPA)
220 East 42nd St., New York, NY 10017
website: http://www.unfpa.org

UNFPA is the largest internationally funded source of population assistance to developing countries. The fund assists developing countries, at their request, in ensuring access to reproductive health services and in devising population and development strategies. It also works to raise awareness of these issues in all countries. Its publications include the report *6 Billion: A Time for Choices* and the yearly *State of the World Population.*

Worldwatch Institute
1776 Massachusetts Ave. NW, Washington, DC 20036
(202) 452-1999
website: http://www.worldwatch.org

The institute is an interdisciplinary research organization that works to inform policy makers and the public about global and environmental issues, including the effects of overpopulation. It publishes the bimonthly *World Watch* magazine, periodic *Worldwatch Papers*, and the annual *State of the World* report.

Zero Population Growth (ZPG)
1400 16th St. NW, Suite 320, Washington, DC 20036
(202) 332-2200
website: http://www.zpg.org

ZPG works to slow population growth and achieve a sustainable balance of population, resources, and the environment. Its education and advocacy programs aim to influence public policies, attitudes, and behavior on national and global population issues and related concerns. It publishes reports and activist kits on issues such as women's access to reproductive services, population and the environment, and religious opposition to population control.

Bibliography of Books

Virginia Abernathy — *Population Politics: The Choices That Shape Our Future.* New York: Plenum Press, 1993.

Philip Appleman — *An Essay on the Principle of Population: Thomas Robert Malthus.* New York: W.W. Norton, 1976.

Asoka Bandarage — *Women, Population, and Global Crisis: A Political-Economic Analysis.* London: Zed Books, 1997.

Leon F. Bouvier and Lindsay Grant — *How Many Americans? Population, Immigration, and the Environment.* San Francisco: Sierra Club Books, 1995.

Peter Brimelow — *Alien Nation: Common Sense About America's Immigration Disaster.* New York: Random House, 1995.

Lester Brown and Gary Gardner — *Beyond Malthus: Nineteen Dimensions of the Population Challenge.* New York: W.W. Norton, 1999.

Robert Cassen et al. — *Population and Development: Old Debates, New Conclusions.* New Brunswick, NJ: Transaction Publishers, 1994.

Stephen Castles and Mark J. Miller — *The Age of Migration: International Population Movements in the Modern World.* New York: Guilford Press, 1998.

Nazli Choucri — *Multidisciplinary Perspectives on Population and Conflict.* Syracuse, NY: Syracuse University Press, 1984.

Robert Cliquet and Kristian Thienpoint — *Population and Development: A Message from the Cairo Conference.* Boston: Kluwer Academic Publishers, 1995.

Joel E. Cohen — *How Many People Can the Earth Support?* New York: W.W. Norton, 1995.

Sonia Correa — *Population and Reproductive Rights: Feminist Perspectives from the South.* London: Zed Books, 1994.

Harold Coward — *Population, Consumption, and the Environment: Religious and Secular Responses.* Albany: State University of New York Press, 1995.

Helen Daugherty and Kenneth Kammeyer — *An Introduction to Population.* New York: Guilford Press, 1995.

Ruth Dixon-Mueller — *Population Policy and Women's Rights: Transforming Reproductive Choice.* Westport, CT: Praeger, 1993.

Alan Thein Durning and Christopher D. Crowther — *Misplaced Blame: The Real Roots of Population Growth*. Seattle: Northwest Environment Watch, 1997.

Tim M. Dyson — *Population and Food: Global Trends and Future Prospects*. New York: Routledge, 1996.

Gregg Easterbrook — *A Moment on the Earth: The Coming Age of Environmental Optimism*. New York: Penguin Books, 1995.

Paul Ehrlich and Anne H. Ehrlich — *The Population Explosion*. New York: Simon & Schuster, 1990.

Paul R. Ehrlich, Anne H. Ehrlich, and Grechen C. Daily — *The Stork and the Plow: The Equity Answer to the Human Dilemma*. New York: Putnam's, 1995.

Michael Fix and Jeffrey S. Passel — *Immigration and Immigrants: Setting the Record Straight*. Washington, DC: Urban Institute, 1994.

Robert W. Fox and Ira H. Mehlman — *Crowding Out the Future: World Population Growth, U.S. Immigration, and Pressures on Natural Resources*. Washington, DC: Federation for American Immigration Reform, 1992.

Robert Goodland, Herman Daly, and Salah El Serafy — *Population, Technology, and Lifestyle*. Covelo, CA: Island Press, 1992.

Lindsey Grant — *Juggernaut: Growth on a Finite Planet*. Santa Ana, CA: Seven Locks Press, 1996.

Garrett Hardin — *Living Within Limits: Ecology, Economics, and Population Taboos*. New York: Oxford University Press, 1995.

Garrett Hardin — *The Ostrich Factor: Population Myopia*. New York: Oxford University Press, 1999.

Betsy Hartmann — *Reproductive Rights and Wrongs: The Global Politics of Population Control*. Boston: South End Press, 1995.

William G. Hollingsworth — *Ending the Explosion: Population Policies and Ethics for a Humane Future*. Santa Ana, CA: Seven Locks Press, 1996.

John Isbister — *The Immigration Debate: Remaking America*. West Hartford, CT: Kumarian Press, 1996.

Janice Jiggins — *Changing the Boundaries: Women-Centered Perspectives on Population and the Environment*. Washington, DC: Island Press, 1994.

Klaus Leesinger and Karin Schmitt — *All Our People: Population Policy with a Human Face*. Washington, DC: Island Press, 1994.

Elizabeth Liagin — *Excessive Force: Power, Politics, and Population Control*. Washington, DC: The Project, 1996.

Massimo Livi-Bacci and Gustavo Dee Santis	*Population and Poverty in the Developing World.* New York: Clarendon Press, 1999.
Wolfgang Lutz	*The Future Population of the World: What Can We Assume Today?* London: Earthscan, 1996.
Daniel C. Maguire, Larry L. Rasmussen, and Rosemary Reuther	*Ethics for a Small Planet: New Horizons on Population, Consumption, and Ecology.* Albany: State University of New York Press, 1998.
Karen L. Michaelson	*And the Poor Get Children: Radical Perspectives on Population Dynamics.* New York: Monthly Review Press, 1981.
George D. Moffett	*Critical Masses: The Global Population Challenge.* New York: Viking, 1994.
Charles B. Nam	*Understanding Population Change.* Itasca, IL: Peacock, 1994.
Gerard Piel	*Only One World: Ours to Make and Keep.* New York: W.H. Freeman, 1992.
Population Action International	*Why Population Matters, 1996.* Washington, DC: Population Action International, 1996.
John F. Rohe	*A Bicentennial Malthusian Essay: Conservation, Population, and the Indifference to Limits.* Traverse City, MI: Rhodes & Easton, 1997.
Jonas Salk	*World Population and Human Values: A New Reality.* New York: Harper and Row, 1981.
John C. Schwarz	*Global Population from a Catholic Perspective.* Mystic, CT: Twenty-Third Century Books, 1998.
Gita Sen and Adrianne Germain	*Population Policies Reconsidered: Health, Empowerment, and Rights.* Cambridge, MA: Harvard University Press, 1994.
Jael Silliman and Ynestra King	*Dangerous Intersections: Feminist Perspectives on Population, Environment, and Development.* Boston: South End Press, 1999.
Julian Simon	*Population Matters: People, Resources, Environment, and Immigration.* New Brunswick, NJ: Transaction Publishers, 1990.
Julian Simon	*The Ultimate Resource 2.* Princeton, NJ: Princeton University Press, 1996.
Michael S. Teitelbaum and Jay Winter	*A Question of Numbers: High Migration, Low Fertility, and the Politics of National Identity.* New York: Hill & Wang, 1998.
Michael Tobias	*World War III: Population and the Biosphere at the End of the Millennium.* New York: Continuum, 1998.
Ben Wattenberg	*The Birth Dearth.* New York: Pharos Books, 1987.

Index

219